"
Nothing ever tasted
better than a cold beer
on a beautiful afternoon
with nothing to look
forward to than more
of the same.
"

HUGH HOOD
ESSAYIST, PROFESSOR

BEER*MISCUOUS*
2812 North Lincoln Avenue
Chicago, IL 60657

beermiscuous.com

ISBN: 978-0-9989958-1-6

Printed in PRC

BEERMISCUOUS
FIELD GUIDE

THE ULTIMATE ADVENTURER'S GUIDE TO
CRAFT BREWERY TAPROOMS + BREWPUBS

BEERMISCUOUS
A Chicago craft beer cafe and bottle shop.

Timothy Musho

BEER*MISCUOUS* Adventures
. . . beyond the café.

Beermiscuous, by definition, is about exploring craft beer. Always respecting your favorites, but no longer being tied solely to them. Having a constant desire to seek out new beers and styles, willing to take risks.

We opened our unique Chicago "coffee shop for beer" in 2014 with the mission of providing the ultimate destination for beer exploration in a welcoming environment that blended European café elegance with the edge of an American coffee shop. But, along our personal journey, we've come to appreciate how valuable and invigorating it is to travel to the source. A visit to a taproom or brewpub provides the freshest beer and insight into the community the brewery has cultivated around its beer.

Our hope is that this field guide will simplify your journey to Chicago's taprooms and brewpubs*, enhance your experiences, and of course, remind you of home (Beermiscuous).

*NOTE: this guide is NOT a comprehensive list of ALL Chicago breweries, only those where you can drink on the site where the beer is brewed.

CONTRIBUTORS

Mindy Dunn (design)

Andrew Hilsberg (research, editing)

Austin Harvey (content)

Paul Leamon (editing, publishing)

TABLE OF CONTENTS

———

REVOLUTION BREWING

FIELD NOTES

3340 N. Kedzie Ave.
Chicago, IL 60618
773-588-2267
revbrew.com

Illinois's largest independently-owned brewery, Revolution is the brainchild of Josh Deth, who opened the eclectic restaurant Handlebar in Wicker Park in 2003. In 2010, Deth became a Logan Square trailblazer by launching a Revolution brewpub on Milwaukee Avenue. The success of that space led to the construction of a large production facility and second taproom on Kedzie. By 2017, Revolution was among the 40 largest craft brewers in the country. A visit to one of Revolution's two taprooms is a must.

OWNER
Josh Deth

HEAD BREWER
Jim Cibak, Wil Turner

AVAILABILITY
IL, IN, MA, MI, NJ, NY, OH, WI

BEST KNOWN FOR
IPAs, lighter styles

DATE FOUNDED
2010

2017 PRODUCTION
82,531 bbl

RECENT AWARDS
FoBAB 2016, 2017, WBC 2016

PUBLIC TRANSIT
'L' Blue/Belmont

16 | 281 | | | • | | • | | | • | 4.1/5

AT-A-GLANCE INFORMATION

| # of taps | seating capacity | outdoor seating | pet friendly | kid friendly | TVs | snacks | full menu | off-street parking | transit friendly | rating |

HOW TO USE THIS GUIDE IN THE FIELD

REVOLUTION BREWING

PRO TIPS

PRO TIPS
A compilation of beer travelers' advice that will help maximize the enjoyment of your visit.

» Visit the brewpub location at: 2323 N. Milwaukee Ave., Chicago, IL.

» Very large industrial space with barrels in the taproom and an excellent view into the brewery.

» Free street parking is easy.

» The 2013 movie "Drinking Buddies" starring Olivia Wilde, Jake Johnson and Anna Kendrick was primarily filmed at the Kedzie taproom.

» While Kedzie is the main production house, Revolution's brewpub features a fantastic food menu and plenty of bike parking out front.

» Even if you're familiar with Revolution's core lineup, both the taproom and the brewpub feature new beer releases and special events each week. Don't miss out!

DATE OF VISIT:

MY RATING
☆ ☆ ☆ ☆ ☆

NOTES:

JOURNAL
A true field guide wouldn't be complete without your own notes on your visit and experiences.

POPULAR BEERS

POPULAR BEERS
Represents a few of the most checked-in beers on social media. May not be available year-round.

ANTI-HERO

FIST CITY

SUN CRUSHER

A LITTLE CRAZY

M	Tu	W	Th	F	S	Su
closed	closed	2-10p	2-10p	2-11p	12-11p	12-6p

HOURS
We advise double checking the hours as these do change frequently.

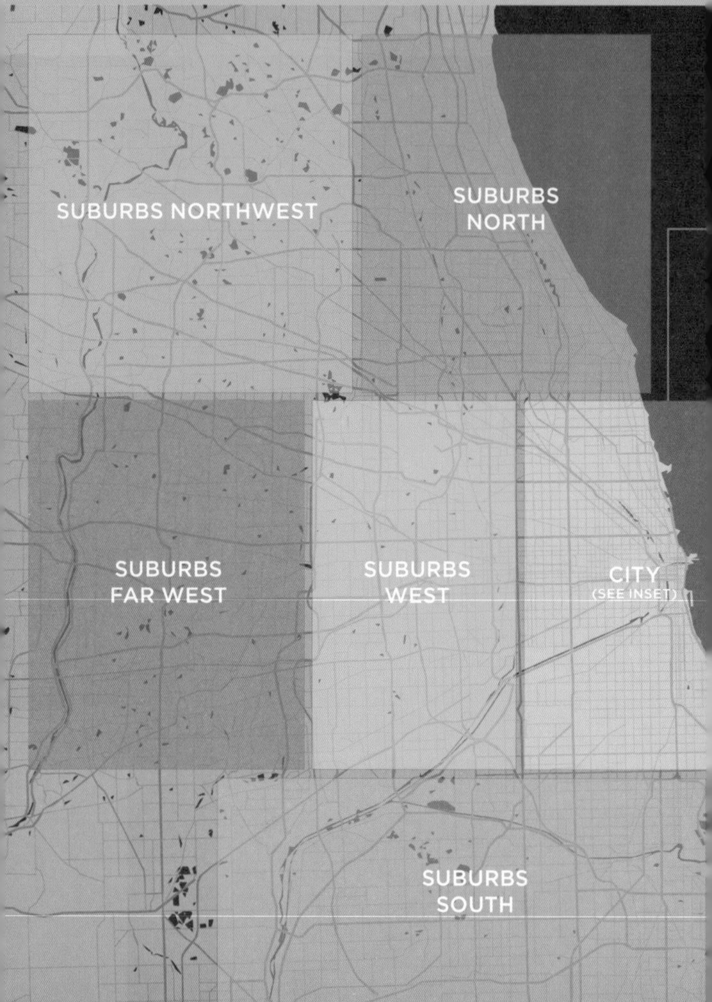

SUBURBS NORTHWEST

SUBURBS NORTH

SUBURBS FAR WEST

SUBURBS WEST

CITY
(SEE INSET)

SUBURBS SOUTH

NEIGHBORHOODS

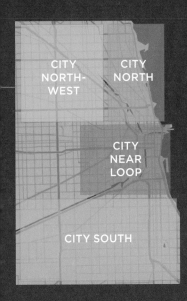

CITY NORTH-WEST

CITY NORTH

CITY NEAR LOOP

CITY SOUTH

SUBURBS
ORTHWEST
INDIANA

In order to simplify your exploration (and stay true to the identity of Chicago as a community of well defined neighborhoods), we've organized the taprooms and brewpubs by similar geography. Take note that each neighborhood is color coded, which corresponds to the colored stripe along the top of each page.

Additionally, each neighborhood chapter begins with a more detailed map of each area. While the maps do provide some basic road detail, they are not meant to be used for directions. We recommend you use them to help plan out possible stops at two or three taprooms/brewpubs in close proximity to each other. Take advantage of your journey.

Enjoy exploring, be safe, and stay beermiscuous!

CITY NORTH

1. Andersonville
2. Band of Bohemia
3. Begyle
4. Burnt City
5. Corridor
6. Dovetail
7. DryHop
8. Empirical
9. Greenstar
10. Half Acre
11. Spiteful

NEIGHBORHOOD HIGHLIGHTS

- Beermiscuous
1. Lincoln Park Zoo
2. Montrose Beach
3. Wrigley Field
4. Old Town School of Folk Music
5. Aragon Ballroom

ANDERSONVILLE BREWING

FIELD NOTES

5402 N. Clark St.
Chicago, IL 60640
773-784-6969
**hamburgermarys.
com/chicago/
brewing/**

The purple-and-pink outside of Hamburger Mary's at the corner of Balmoral and Clark is unmistakable, as is the winking lady holding up a massive burger on a plate in the style of your favorite Frisch's or Big Boy diner. This neighborhood burger joint is more than just a place for folks to "Eat, Drink, and be Mary," though. The self-proclaimed "oldest nano-brewery in Chicago," Andersonville Brewing, dates back to 2009 and is the craft brew project of Hamburger Mary's, a longtime mainstay in the Andersonville neighborhood.

OWNER
Brandon Wright,
Ashley Wright

HEAD BREWER
Brandon Wright

AVAILABILITY
Brewpub only

BEST KNOWN FOR
IPAs, sessionable
ales

DATE FOUNDED
2009

2017 PRODUCTION
135 bbl

16 | 76 | • | | • | • | | • | | | 3.3/5

ANDERSONVILLE BREWING

PRO TIPS

» Many beer-themed ingredients featured on the food menu, from the gravy in the poutine to the BBQ sauce.

» A rotating IPA is always available for the hop-heads; barrel-aged beers now and then.

» Advertises as being "one of just a few certified GREEN restaurants in Chicago."

» Kitchen closes a few hours before the bar.

» Weekend brunch available until 3p.

» The Attic, usually open Wednesdays-Sundays, was named one of the best gay bars in the world by OUT Magazine, with live music, cabaret, and dance parties.

POPULAR BEERS

DATE OF VISIT:

MY RATING

NOTES:

M	Tu	W	Th	F	S	Su
5p-12a	5p-12a	5p-12a	5p-1:30	5p-1:30	12-2:30	12p-12a

BAND OF BOHEMIA

FIELD NOTES

4710 N. Ravenswood Ave.
Chicago, IL 60640
773-271-4710
bandofbohemia.com

The first brewpub to ever win a coveted Michelin star, Band of Bohemia has the most integrated food-and-beer program of any restaurant in the city, perhaps the country. Head brewer and co-founder Michael Carroll began as a chef, working in New England before landing at Chicago's legendary Alinea restaurant in 2006. Half Acre brought him on as a brewer in 2009, and since then his passions and talents have led him to create beers meant to specifically pair with dishes, creating a special dining experience that few restaurants in the world can offer.

OWNER
Craig Sindelar,
Michael Carroll

HEAD BREWER
Michael Carroll

AVAILABILITY
Chicago - limited

BEST KNOWN FOR
Food inspired ales
with spices and
fruits

DATE FOUNDED
2015

RECENT AWARDS
Michelin starred

KEY EVENTS
Caravan Art Festival
(Sept)

PUBLIC TRANSIT
'L' Brown/Damen,
UP-N/Ravenswood

| 8 | 150 | | | • | | | • | • | | 3.8/5 |

BAND OF BOHEMIA

PRO TIPS

- » Features a pre-fixe, multi-course meal with beers spotlighting adjunct spices designed to pair with each course.
- » Not your typical brewery/brewpub.
- » Atmosphere is almost akin to a fancy Viennese salon, featuring artwork by Chicago artist Elizabeth Weber.
- » Upscale but approachable and unpretentious.
- » While reservations aren't required, we recommend making one.
- » There are specific times the kitchen is closed but the bar is open, so double check hours ahead of time if you're hoping to eat.

DATE OF VISIT:

MY RATING
☆ ☆ ☆ ☆ ☆

NOTES:

POPULAR BEERS

Orange Chicory Rye	The Culinary Noble

M	Tu	W	Th	F	S	Su
closed	4:30-12	4:30-12	4:30-12	4:30-12	10a-1a	10-10p

BEGYLE BREWING CO.

FIELD NOTES

Begyle is one of many breweries that occupy former industrial buildings along the railroad tracks on Ravenswood Avenue in the North Center neighborhood, an area that has been branded Malt Row. One of the original breweries in the corridor, Begyle started solely as a subscription-based CSB (community supported brewery), delivering fresh-brewed growlers to customers. The opening of their taproom in 2015, along with their approachable flagship beers, has since made them a neighborhood staple.

1800 W. Cuyler Ave.
Chicago, IL 60613
773-661-6963
begylebrewing.com

OWNER
Kevin Cary

HEAD BREWER
Liz French

AVAILABILITY
IL, MI

BEST KNOWN FOR
Classic American styles, barrel-aged specialties

DATE FOUNDED
2012

2017 PRODUCTION
3,500 bbl

KEY EVENTS
BA Imperial Pajamas Release (Nov); Mayfestiversary; Oktoberfestiversary

PUBLIC TRANSIT
'L' Brown/Irving Park

13 | 60 | | • | • | | • | | | • | 4.0/5

BEGYLE BREWING CO.

PRO TIPS

» The taproom is small and welcoming with a coffee shop vibe. When things get crowded, the brewery is opened up for additional standing space.

» Food trucks and pop-ups most weekends.

» Tours are on Saturdays at noon. $10 gets you a 90 minute tour, three pours and a Begyle glass.

» Begyle's Skeeball room is home to a single machine that sees plenty of use, and even hosts a Skeeball league.

» An upstairs event space allows for both private and public events.

» Pair with a visit to Dovetail, just a block away.

DATE OF VISIT:

MY RATING
☆ ☆ ☆ ☆ ☆

NOTES:

POPULAR BEERS

M	Tu	W	Th	F	S	Su
12-9p	12-9p	12-9p	12-9p	12-10p	11a-12a	12-8p

BURNT CITY BREWING

FIELD NOTES

2747 N. Lincoln Ave.
Chicago, IL 60614
773-295-1270
burntcitybrewing.com

Referencing the Great Chicago Fire of 1871, Burnt City Brewing is the continuation of what was Atlas Brewing. Founded in 2012, Atlas was forced to change names in 2015, and the phoenix that rose from those ashes was Burnt City. Head pub brewer Christian Burd supplements a list of several perennial beers brewed in their south side Chicago production brewery with some uniquely marvelous creations at the pub. Knowing the neighborhood of younger professionals and exuberant craft beer novices, Burd isn't afraid of fruit beers, either.

OWNER
John Saller, Ben Saller

HEAD BREWER
Christian Burd

AVAILABILITY
AL, IL, IN

BEST KNOWN FOR
Saisons, wheat ales

DATE FOUNDED
2012

KEY EVENTS
Craft Beer Prom (May), New Year's Eve Party (Dec)

PUBLIC TRANSIT
'L' Brown/Diversey

25 | 200 | • | | • | • | | • | | • | 3.6/5

BURNT CITY BREWING

PRO TIPS

» The connected lounge is a stylish, hip bowling alley that allows you a way to burn off the beer you consume and impress your friends.

» Features upscale takes on classic pub fare, including totchos (think nachos, but with tater tots replacing the tortilla chips), fried pickles, pizzas (try the white pizza with stout-braised mushrooms) and BBQ (the burnt ends go great with a barrel-aged brew).

» Production brewery is on the south side of Chicago and does not offer tours or a taproom.

» Pair with a visit to your favorite Chicago craft beer bar: Beermiscuous (just steps away)!

DATE OF VISIT:

MY RATING
☆ ☆ ☆ ☆ ☆

NOTES:

POPULAR BEERS

M	Tu	W	Th	F	S	Su
5-11p	5-11p	5-11p	5-11p	5-2a	12p-2a	12-11p

CORRIDOR BREWERY & PROVISIONS

FIELD NOTES

3446 N. Southport Ave.
Chicago, IL 60657
773-270-4272
corridorchicago.com

The sister pub to East Lakeview's DryHop Brewers, Corridor Brewery & Provisions resides on the western side of Lakeview in a neighborhood known as the Southport Corridor. Perhaps a little more upscale than DryHop, Corridor is the place to go if you want a classy atmosphere for a meal with the family or a date night. The brewery gained considerable buzz in 2017 for their impressive lineup of Double Dry-Hopped IPAs, some of the best juicy, hazy IPAs you'll find in the city.

OWNER
Greg Shuff

HEAD BREWER
Roger Cuzelis

AVAILABILITY
Brewpub only

BEST KNOWN FOR
DDA Hazy IPAs, saisons, fruit-forward beers

DATE FOUNDED
2015

2017 PRODUCTION
1,000 bbl

RECENT AWARDS
GABF 2017

KEY EVENTS
Anniversary Party (Oct)

PUBLIC TRANSIT
'L' Brown/Southport

| 6 | 90 | • | • | • | | | • | | • | 3.9/5 |

CORRIDOR BREWERY & PROVISIONS

PRO TIPS

» Dog friendly on the patio only.

» No reservations are taken, so show up early or plan to wait if you're coming during the evening, weekend or brunch.

» The menu features multiple mussels dishes, clay-oven pizzas, sandwiches and salads, all lovingly considered.

» On Mondays, you can get their burger, a pint and a shot for $15. Every Saturday they have $5 crowler/$7 growler fills for one specific beer.

» Weekly Tuesday Beer & Vinyl events.

» Pair with a concert at Schubas, movies at the Music Box or shopping at the boutiques along Southport Avenue.

DATE OF VISIT:

MY RATING
☆ ☆ ☆ ☆ ☆

NOTES:

POPULAR BEERS

| Wizard Fight | Squeezlt | Cosmic Juicebox | Bendy Straw |

M	Tu	W	Th	F	S	Su
11a-11p	11a-11p	11a-12a	11a-12a	11a-12a	10a-12a	10a-11p

DOVETAIL BREWERY

FIELD NOTES

1800 W. Belle Plaine Ave.
Chicago, IL 60613
773-683-1414
dovetailbrewery.com

Dovetail is the brainchild of Hagen Dost and Bill Wesselink, who came up with the idea as they studied brewing at the Doemens Akademie in Munich. Dovetail's choice of locating in an old industrial building is a stellar fit since the ideals of high-quality manufacturing craftsmanship are applied to the brewing process here. In fact, the brewery features a copper vessel repurposed from the pilot system at Weihenstephan in Bavaria, the world's oldest continuously-functioning brewery.

OWNER
Hagen Dost, Bill Wesselink

HEAD BREWER
Hagen Dost, Bill Wesselink

AVAILABILITY
IL, IN

BEST KNOWN FOR
German style lagers, wheat ales

DATE FOUNDED
2015

2017 PRODUCTION
1,100 bbl

KEY EVENTS
Mayfestiversary (May), Oktoberfestiversary (Oct)

PUBLIC TRANSIT
'L' Brown/Irving Park

18 | 90 | • | • | • | | | • | | | • | • | 4.1/5

DOVETAIL BREWERY

PRO TIPS

» Outdoor picnic tables are only available on Saturday and Sunday.

» Take the brewery tour here Saturdays at 11a. The copper vessel from Germany and the story behind it, are both fascinating and worth every moment of time spent talking about it.

» House-blended radlers are available that marry house beers with light sodas. If you're feeling adventurous, try the Rauchbier (smoked beer), or better yet, try a radler made with it. You've never had anything like it before.

» Food trucks come by occasionally.

» Large private event space available.

» Located on Malt Row in Ravenwood. Pair with a visit to Begyle.

DATE OF VISIT:

MY RATING
☆ ☆ ☆ ☆ ☆

NOTES:

POPULAR BEERS

Lager	Hefewei-zen	Rauch-bier	Dunkel-weizen

M	Tu	W	Th	F	S	Su
4-7p	12-10p	12-10p	12-10p	12-11p	11a-11p	12-8p

DRYHOP BREWERS

FIELD NOTES

3155 N. Broadway
Chicago, IL 60657
773-857-3155
dryhopchicago.com

DryHop is located not far from the Boystown area of Lakeview, one of the first municipally-recognized gay neighborhoods anywhere in the country. There's plenty of foot traffic in this area that has a bevy of restaurants, bars, boutiques and independently-owned businesses. DryHop is only a mile away from Wrigley Field and it has quickly become a neighborhood landmark thanks to its well-regarded food menu and frequent beer releases and collaborations.

OWNER
Greg Shuff

HEAD BREWER
Eric Padilla

AVAILABILITY
Brewpub only

BEST KNOWN FOR
West Coast IPAs, APAs, stouts

DATE FOUNDED
2013

2017 PRODUCTION
1,000 bbl

KEY EVENTS
Anniversary Party (Jun)

PUBLIC TRANSIT
'L' Red, Brown or Purple/Belmont

6 | 75 | • | • | • | | | • | | • | 3.8/5

DRYHOP BREWERS

PRO TIPS

» Dog friendly on the patio only.

» When the windows and patio are open here, DryHop seems like the coolest place in town.

» Growler Saturday Special rotates each week: $5 crowler, $7 growler.

» DryHop's sister pub, Corridor Brewery & Provisions, is just a mile west.

» Not a lot of seating and the bar area is very small. Expect to wait a bit when the sun is shining and people are out and about.

» Director of Brewing Operations Brant Dubovick is a decorated brewmaster with over a decade of experience and a GABF gold medal on his résumé.

DATE OF VISIT:

MY RATING
☆ ☆ ☆ ☆ ☆

NOTES:

POPULAR BEERS

| Shark Meets Hipster | Milksta-chio | The Angry Samoan | Victorian Flavour |

M	Tu	W	Th	F	S	Su
11a-12a	11a-12a	11a-12a	11a-12a	11a-2a	11a-2a	11a-12a

EMPIRICAL BREWERY

FIELD NOTES

Science-themed brews with a nod toward experimentation is the name of the game for Empirical with delightfully drinkable results. Each Thursday they release a new beer in the taproom direct from their pilot brewing system. This original location in Ravenswood features a cinder block, big TV, and Christmas light vibe that's actually quite charming.

1801 W. Foster Ave.
Chicago, IL 60640
773-654-3104
empiricalbrewery.com

OWNER
Bill Hurley

HEAD BREWER
Jacob Huston

AVAILABILITY
Chicago

BEST KNOWN FOR
Experimental
varieties

DATE FOUNDED
2014

KEY EVENTS
Fat Tuesday
Crawfish Boil (Feb),
Black Wednesday
Party (Nov),
Anniversary Party
(Nov)

PUBLIC TRANSIT
'L' Red/Morse

12 | 95 | | • | • | • | • | | | • | 3.9/5

EMPIRICAL BREWERY

PRO TIPS

» Visit their other location at: 1330 W. Morse Ave., Chicago, IL (brewpub).

» While the taproom is still BYOF, use GrubHub and order from Empirical's new brewpub location opened in 2017.

» The taproom is dog friendly (don't worry, the feral cats that brought this taproom a bit of local press are separated away in the brewhouse).

» Brewery tours are every Saturday at 2p, no reservations, and they include a flight and pint glass all for $10.

» Plenty of weekly events like Tuesday Bingo, Build Your Own Flight Wednesday, New Beer Thursday and Firkin Friday.

» Features live music occasionally.

DATE OF VISIT:

MY RATING
☆ ☆ ☆ ☆ ☆

NOTES:

POPULAR BEERS

Cold Fusion Cream Ale	Symbiotic Sour	Proton No Coast IPA	Electron SMaSH

M	Tu	W	Th	F	S	Su
closed	12-10p	12-10p	12p-12a	12p-12a	12p-12a	12p-8p

GREENSTAR BREWING

FIELD NOTES

3800 N. Clark St.
Chicago, IL 60013
773-929-3680
**uncommonground.
com/green-
star-brewing**

Uncommon Ground/Greenstar Brewing, in the Wrigleyville neighborhood, is a bit of an anomaly in an area that can get absolutely bonkers on game days. This classy restaurant and bar a couple of blocks north of Wrigley Field is a destination for the neighborhood's population of young professionals and Cubs fans looking for a more laid-back game day experience. As a natural extension to their local, organic and sustainable ideals, Uncommon Ground launched the 7-barrel brewery Greenstar in 2014, as the first certified organic brewery in Illinois.

OWNER
Michael Cameron,
Helen Cameron

HEAD BREWER
Martin Coad

AVAILABILITY
Brewpub only

BEST KNOWN FOR
IPAs, pales, stouts,
Kölsch

DATE FOUNDED
2014

KEY EVENTS
Oktoberfest
(Sept), 12 Beers of
Christmas (Dec)

PUBLIC TRANSIT
'L' Red/Addison

12 | 150 | • | • | • | | | • | | • | 3.5/5

GREENSTAR BREWING

PRO TIPS

» Dog friendly on the patio only.

» What Greenstar's beers might lack in bonkers experimentalism they more than make up for in environmental and food-friendliness.

» Operates two independently-owned restaurants in the city. A second Uncommon Ground location is in Edgewater at 1401 West Devon Avenue, not far from Loyola University. These are the only two locations where you'll find Greenstar.

» The food menu has plenty of vegetarian and vegan options, as well as some gluten-free dishes.

» Very popular weekend brunch.

» Located steps away from two premier music venues: Metro and Smart Bar.

POPULAR BEERS

Space-ship IPA	Mutti's	Monk's Libation	Certifi-able Pale Ale

DATE OF VISIT:

MY RATING

NOTES:

M	Tu	W	Th	F	S	Su
11a-9p	11a-9p	11a-9p	11a-9p	11a-11p	9a-11p	9a-11p

HALF ACRE BEER CO.

FIELD NOTES

4257 N. Lincoln Ave.
Chicago, IL 60618
773-248-4038
halfacrebeer.com

Brew Bokeh

Around for more than 10 years, Half Acre now qualifies as one of the old guard of Chicago craft beer. Half Acre started by contract brewing in Wisconsin and opened their original Lincoln Avenue production facility in 2008. It was several years before they added a taproom and a few more until a kitchen was added. Exponential growth fueled by popular beers like Daisy Cutter led Half Acre to build a second production facility on Balmoral Avenue in Bowmanville. A long-awaited larger taproom opened there in 2017 with an outdoor beer garden. Bottom line: visit Half Acre and pay tribute to an O.G.

OWNER
Gabriel Magliaro, Matt Gallagher, Maurizio Fiori, Brian Black

HEAD BREWER
Matt Young

AVAILABILITY
IL, WI, Philadelphia, New York City

BEST KNOWN FOR
Pales, IPAs

DATE FOUNDED
2006

RECENT AWARDS
FoBAB 2016

KEY EVENTS
Big North (Aug), Big Hugs Release (Dec)

PUBLIC TRANSIT
'L' Brown/Montrose

14 | 70 | | | | • | | | • | | | • | 4.1/5

HALF ACRE BEER CO.

PRO TIPS

» Visit their other location at: 2050 W. Balmoral, Chicago, IL (taproom+beer garden).

» Lincoln is likely to be loud and crowded, but that's its appeal. Join a group in the beer hall-style seating and make new friends.

» At Lincoln, tasty burritos get a culinary twist while the "science cheese" of their now-famous nachos puts the gooey ballpark stuff to shame.

» Balmoral is more chef-driven with dishes like pâté, salmon and pork ribs. Don't skip the house made bread or Sunday brunch.

» Explore with your beer picks. Half Acre pretty much nails every style.

» Pair a visit to the Balmoral taproom with Spiteful next door.

POPULAR BEERS

M	Tu	W	Th	F	S	Su
closed	11a-11p	11a-11p	11a-12a	11a-1a	11a-1a	11a-11p

Brew Bokeh

DATE OF VISIT:

MY RATING
☆ ☆ ☆ ☆ ☆

NOTES:

SPITEFUL BREWING

FIELD NOTES

Chicago, IL

2024 W. Balmoral Ave
Chicago, IL 60625
773-293-6600
spitefulbrewing.com

One of the wonders of Chicago craft beer is how Spiteful managed to churn out as much beer as they did for five years out of their previous miniscule location in North Center. The new facility in Bowmanville greatly expands their capacity, allows the brewers much more freedom to experiment with styles, and provides a long-awaited taproom for fans. And demonstrating the spirit of camaraderie in Chicago's beer industry, they've been warmly welcomed by their neighbors, Half Acre, who opened a second taproom location next door a few months earlier in 2017.

OWNER
Brad Shaffer, Jason Klein

HEAD BREWER
Brad Shaffer

AVAILABILITY
IL

BEST KNOWN FOR
IPAs, stouts, porters

DATE FOUNDED
2012

RECENT AWARDS
FoBAB 2016

16 | 84 | | • | • | | • | | | | 4.3/5

SPITEFUL BREWING

PRO TIPS

» The focus here is on the beer. The stylish wood bar seats over a dozen and there are a variety of table seating options. Spiteful beer label art adorns the walls.

» During periods of warmer weather, the garage-style doors of the Spiteful taproom can be thrown open to provide an outdoor feel.

» Don't let the quiet neighborhood setting fool you. While the bar can get a bit crowded during weekend afternoons, it never seems unfriendly or unmanageable.

» Owners Jason Klein and Brad Shaffer are north suburban childhood buddies who grew up playing hockey together.

DATE OF VISIT:

MY RATING
☆ ☆ ☆ ☆ ☆

NOTES:

POPULAR BEERS

M	Tu	W	Th	F	S	Su
closed	closed	4-10p	4-10p	12p-12a	11a-12a	11a-10p

CITY NORTHWEST

1. Alarmist
2. Eris
3. Hopewell
4. Maplewood
5. Metropolitan
6. Old Irving
7. Piece
8. Revolution

NEIGHBORHOOD HIGHLIGHTS

1 The 606 Trail
2 Bang Bang Pie Shop
3 Basilica of St. Hyacinth
4 Irish American Heritage Center

7

1

North

ALARMIST BREWING

FIELD NOTES

4055 W. Peterson Ave.
Chicago, IL 60646
773-681-0877
alarmistbrewing.com

Gary Gulley started with homebrewing over 25 years ago, but his passion only fully took hold of him in 2015. Opting more for quality over quantity, Alarmist has been perfecting recipes on their core lines of beers as opposed to producing as many beers in as many possible styles as they can. Their taproom space in the formerly dry Sauganash neighborhood occupies the former site of the Siebel Institute of Technology, North America's premier brewing school.

OWNER
Gary Gulley

DATE FOUNDED
2015

HEAD BREWER
Aaron Dahl

AVAILABILITY
Chicago

BEST KNOWN FOR
IPAs, pales, Belgian singles

| 12 | 70 | | | • | | • | | | | • | | 4.0/5 |

ALARMIST BREWING

PRO TIPS

» The Sauganash neighborhood has an almost-suburban feel to it.

» For cyclists, the brewery is right off the Sauganash Trail, a re-purposed 1-mile railway bridge that goes between Devon and Bryn Mawr Avenues. The North Branch (on the west of Alarmist) and North Shore Channel (on the east) bike trails are both within reasonable distances from Alarmist.

» Taproom now accepts cash, credit and Apple Pay.

» Alarmist's latest brewing experiments include hazy, New England-style IPAs, including Juguito, a Mexican hot chocolate-inspired brew with cacao, cayenne, cinnamon, and vanilla.

DATE OF VISIT:

MY RATING
☆ ☆ ☆ ☆ ☆

NOTES:

POPULAR BEERS

   Les Jus Hazy IPA

M	Tu	W	Th	F	S	Su
4-11p	4-11p	4-11p	4-11p	12p-12a	11a-12a	12-10p

ERIS BREWERY & CIDER HOUSE

FIELD NOTES

4240 W. Irving Park Rd.
Chicago, IL 60641
773-943-6200
erischicago.com

Eris opened in 2018 in the Old Irving Park neighborhood right off the Kennedy Expressway. Co-owner Michelle Foik has plenty of experience in Chicago's beer industry, having worked at the Goose Island brewpubs, as well as helping Revolution open in Logan Square. Teaming with Katy Pizza, these women have lovingly repurposed an old building into a beautiful and modern vaulted space that still feels cozy enough for families and friendly enough for the neighborhood crowd looking to enjoy a bite and a drink after a hard day's work.

OWNER
Michelle Foik,
Katy Pizza

HEAD BREWER
Hayley Shine

AVAILABILITY
Brewpub only

BEST KNOWN FOR
Session ales,
vegetable inspired
beers, crisp ciders

DATE FOUNDED
2018

KEY EVENTS
Groundhog Day
(Feb)

PUBLIC TRANSIT
'L' Blue/Irving Park,
UP-NW/Irving Park

20 | 250 | • | | | • | | | • | • | • | 4.0/5

ERIS BREWERY & CIDER HOUSE

PRO TIPS

» Even though this is a beer guide, do not skip Eris' experimental ciders. Whether it's lavender-infused or a blueberry dry-hopped cider, they know what they're doing.

» The pub can accommodate all types of patrons with the perfect balance of bar seating for singles, countless tables for families and groups and an upstairs party room for larger gatherings.

» The food menu combines comfort foods with healthy alternatives. Bar snacks (popcorn, cheese board) appetizers (beer cheddar dip), salads, sandwiches (bacon-wrapped smoked Polish sausage) and a half-dozen hearty entrées.

POPULAR BEERS

| Foiken Haze | EEPAH | Van Van Mojo (cider) | Blush (cider) |

M	Tu	W	Th	F	S	Su
11a-12a	11a-12a	11a-12a	11a-12a	11-1:30	11-1:30	11a-12a

DATE OF VISIT:

MY RATING
☆ ☆ ☆ ☆ ☆

NOTES:

HOPEWELL BREWING CO.

FIELD NOTES

The influx of young people into Logan Square has meant a lot of thirsty folks clamoring for beer. On the northwest edge of the neighborhood, Hopewell taproom is a nexus for the area's discerning beverage crowd. The main focus of Hopewell Brewing is on balanced, utilitarian beers so don't expect face-puckering, enamel-peeling sours or tongue-lashing, hyper-bitter IPAs. Instead, expect to drink beers here that you wouldn't mind having several of during an afternoon.

2760 N. Milwaukee Ave.
Chicago, IL 60647
773-698-6178
hopewellbrewing.com

OWNER
Jonathan Fritz,
Samantha Lee,
Stephen Bossu

HEAD BREWER
Stephen Bossu

AVAILABILITY
Chicago

BEST KNOWN FOR
Balanced beers,
lagers, IPAs, kettle
sours

DATE FOUNDED
2016

RECENT AWARDS
FoBAB 2016, 2017

KEY EVENTS
Anniversary Party
(Feb), Back to
School Bash (Aug),
Halloween (Oct)

PUBLIC TRANSIT
'L' Blue/Logan
Square

10 | 99 | | • | • | | | | • | 3.8/5

HOPEWELL BREWING CO.

PRO TIPS

» It's a very well lit, bright modern space. Big windows let you look into the brewhouse.

» Crowds will get big on weekends and some nights but the atmosphere is generally accommodating and friendly.

» A few reservations are taken on a day-to-day basis.

» No kitchen, but they usually schedule at least one restaurant pop-up or monthly dinner on the calendar every month.

» A nice selection of board games are available while you drink.

» Perfect spot for a drink before or after a movie at the nearby Logan Theatre.

POPULAR BEERS

M	Tu	W	Th	F	S	Su
closed	4-11p	4-11p	4-11p	4-12a	12p-12a	12p-11p

DATE OF VISIT:

MY RATING
☆ ☆ ☆ ☆ ☆

NOTES:

MAPLEWOOD BREWERY & DISTILLERY

FIELD NOTES

2717 N. Maplewood Ave.
Chicago, IL 60647
773-270-1061
maplewoodbrew.com

Maplewood began as Mercenary Brewing in 2014 as brothers Ari and Paul Megalis teamed up with Adam Cieslak to turn a homebrewing hobby into a full-time gig. A cease-and-desist letter from Odell led to the 2015 name change, which honors the former village of Maplewood and is the avenue on which the brewery stands. Their first major taste of the limelight came in 2016 when their Charlatan Pale Ale took bronze at the Great American Beer Festival. In the past few years, Maplewood has come into its own with Juice Pants, a popular series of hazy IPAs.

OWNER
Adam Cieslak,
Ari Megalis, Paul
Megalis

HEAD BREWER
Adam Cieslak, Ari
Megalis

AVAILABILITY
IL, NW IN, SW MI

BEST KNOWN FOR
Hoppy beers, stouts,
spirits

DATE FOUNDED
2014

RECENT AWARDS
GABF 2016, 2017

KEY EVENTS
Casimir Pulaski Day
(Mar)

14 | 63 | | | | | | • | | | 4.2/5

MAPLEWOOD BREWERY & DISTILLERY

PRO TIPS

» The Maplewood "Lounge" is a hidden gem of sorts. Opened in December 2017, it's tucked into a dead-end street off Diversey in a corner of Logan Square cut off from the rest of the neighborhood by the Kennedy Expressway.

» The space is a hip and cozy nook. The location, lighting and size combine to create a perfect lounge atmosphere.

» The kitchen is open until 10pm, offering burgers, mac & cheese, Publican sausages and corn dogs.

» Maplewood's distillery license means the cocktails on draft and Boozy Slushies (with spirits all made in-house) are must-try items as well.

DATE OF VISIT:

MY RATING
☆ ☆ ☆ ☆ ☆

NOTES:

POPULAR BEERS

M	Tu	W	Th	F	S	Su
closed	4p-12a	4p-12a	4p-12a	4p-12a	12p-2a	11a-12a

METROPOLITAN BREWING

FIELD NOTES

3057 N. Rockwell St.
Chicago, IL 60618
773-754-0494
metrobrewing.com

Metropolitan is the second-oldest production brewery in Chicago behind Goose Island. They were located in the Ravenswood neighborhood for nine years before moving south and west to a new facility with a beautiful taproom on the edge of the North Branch Chicago River. Metropolitan's focus has always been German-style lagers. You'll never find an IPA or even a blonde ale in the mix here, but don't think that flavor is being sacrificed. The beers are consistent and delicious, and have garnered the respect of the entire Chicago craft beer community.

OWNER
Doug Hurst, Tracy Hurst

HEAD BREWER
Doug Hurst

AVAILABILITY
IL, WI

BEST KNOWN FOR
Germal styles, lagers

DATE FOUNDED
2008

KEY AWARDS
WBC 2016

12 | 100 | | • | • | | | | | 4.0/5

METROPOLITAN BREWING

PRO TIPS

» The area around Metropolitan is still under development so follow the signs that direct you back to the taproom. You'll be more than rewarded for your efforts.

» Due to Chicago's industrial history, there aren't many places along the Chicago River that one would call scenic. However, the large windows in Metropolitan's taproom provide a gorgeous view of the river and its surrounding trees.

» There are plenty of seats at the bar and the spacious interior includes plenty of long, beer hall-style tables.

» If you're looking for a craft beer space to host a large reception or event, Metropolitan belongs on your shortlist.

POPULAR BEERS

M	Tu	W	Th	F	S	Su
4-10p	4-10p	4-11p	4-11p	4p-12a	12p-12a	12-10p

DATE OF VISIT:

MY RATING

☆ ☆ ☆ ☆ ☆

NOTES:

OLD IRVING BREWING CO.

FIELD NOTES

4419 W. Montrose Ave.
Chicago, IL 60641
773-916-6421
oldirvingbrewing.com

In a residential neighborhood that is starting to see its fair share of families move in, it's no surprise that a top-notch brewpub would open up in Old Irving Park. It's not often that a brewpub's food is on par with its beer, at least when the beer is this excellent. And yet, Old Irving Brewery's menu is among the best of all brewpubs in the city, with its adventurous-yet-approachable dining options rivaling Trevor Rose-Hamblin's remarkable beers. Many popular Chicago publications seem to wholeheartedly agree.

OWNER
Trevor Rose-Hamblin, Jeff Linnemeyer, Matthias Merges

HEAD BREWER
Trevor Rose-Hamblin

AVAILABILITY
Brewpub, limited draft

BEST KNOWN FOR
Stouts, hazy IPAs, Belgians, lighter ales

DATE FOUNDED
2016

PUBLIC TRANSIT
'L' Blue/Montrose

20 | 225 | | | • | • | | • | | • | 3.9/5

OLD IRVING BREWING CO.

PRO TIPS

» Special bottle releases will happen at the pub every now and then; call in advance to see when the next one is.

» The sandwiches and entrées are all fabulous, but the small plates, like the fried zucchini strips and shishito peppers, are not to be missed.

» Every Monday they have a new featured burger, beer, and bourbon for $15.

» Does not take reservations, so for more popular hours, expect a wait.

» Great place to bring the family. Brewery visible from the dining area.

» 14 TVs and a 10' big screen for just about any sporting event.

» Yoga on select weekend mornings in the brewery.

POPULAR BEERS

DATE OF VISIT:

MY RATING
☆ ☆ ☆ ☆ ☆

NOTES:

M	Tu	W	Th	F	S	Su
5-11p	5-11p	5-11p	5-11p	3p-1a	11a-1a	11a-10p

PIECE BREWERY & PIZZERIA

FIELD NOTES

1927 W. North Ave.
Chicago, IL 60622
773-772-4422
piecechicago.com

Rick Nielsen (guitarist in Rock and Roll Hall of Fame inductee Cheap Trick) is a part owner of this Wicker Park mainstay. Sometimes Nielsen's famous five-necked guitar will be on display in this restaurant with beautiful exposed bow truss architectural features. Brewmaster Jonathan Cutler (no relation to the former Bears' quarterback, which is probably a good thing in this town) has won several deserved awards for his quaffable, flavorful beers that always seem to go well with the New Haven-style pizzas.

OWNER Bill Jacobs	**DATE FOUNDED** 2001
HEAD BREWER Jonathan Cutler	**RECENT AWARDS** GABF 2016, 2017
AVAILABILITY Brewpub only	**KEY EVENTS** Festivus (Nov)
BEST KNOWN FOR Pale ales, German wheat ales, lighter ales	**PUBLIC TRANSIT** 'L' Blue/Damen

16 | 275 | | | • | • | | • | | • | 3.8/5

PIECE BREWERY & PIZZERIA

PRO TIPS

» The pizza here is New Haven-style, which means thin crusts, oblong-shaped pies, and super-hot oven temperatures leading to charred crusts.

» They have brunch pizzas on Saturday and Sunday.

» Don't miss the special pizza of the month with a local "celebrity" like Doug Sohn of now-closed Hot Doug's.

» Fun fact: the Cheetah Gym across the street used to be the home of MTV's The Real World.

» Will get busy during weekend evenings and big sporting events, so don't plan to find a seat immediately.

» Live band karaoke on Saturdays at 11p.

POPULAR BEERS

The Weight	Golden Arm	Camel Toe	Top Heavy Hefeweizen

DATE OF VISIT:

MY RATING
☆ ☆ ☆ ☆ ☆

NOTES:

M	Tu	W	Th	F	S	Su
11a-12a	11a-12a	11a-12a	11a-12a	11a-2a	11a-2a	11a-11p

REVOLUTION BREWING

FIELD NOTES

Illinois's largest independently-owned brewery, Revolution is the brainchild of Josh Deth, who opened the eclectic restaurant Handlebar in Wicker Park in 2003. In 2010, Deth became a Logan Square trailblazer by launching a Revolution brewpub on Milwaukee Avenue. The success of that space led to the construction of a large production facility and second taproom on Kedzie. By 2017, Revolution was among the 40 largest craft brewers in the country. A visit to one of Revolution's two taprooms is a must.

3340 N. Kedzie Ave.
Chicago, IL 60618
773-588-2267
revbrew.com

OWNER
Josh Deth

HEAD BREWER
Jim Cibak, Wil Turner

AVAILABILITY
IL, IN, MA, MI, NJ, NY, OH, WI

BEST KNOWN FOR
IPAs, lighter styles

DATE FOUNDED
2010

2017 PRODUCTION
82,531 bbl

RECENT AWARDS
FoBAB 2016, 2017, WBC 2016

PUBLIC TRANSIT
'L' Blue/Belmont

16 | 281 | | | • | | • | | | • | 4.1/5

REVOLUTION BREWING

PRO TIPS

» Visit the brewpub location at: 2323 N. Milwaukee Ave., Chicago, IL.

» Very large industrial space with barrels in the taproom and an excellent view into the brewery.

» Free street parking is easy.

» The 2013 movie "Drinking Buddies" starring Olivia Wilde, Jake Johnson and Anna Kendrick was primarily filmed at the Kedzie taproom.

» While Kedzie is the main production house, Revolution's brewpub features a fantastic food menu and plenty of bike parking out front.

» Even if you're familiar with Revolution's core lineup, both the taproom and the brewpub feature new beer releases and special events each week. Don't miss out!

POPULAR BEERS

M	Tu	W	Th	F	S	Su
closed	closed	2-10p	2-10p	2-11p	12-11p	12-6p

DATE OF VISIT:

MY RATING

NOTES:

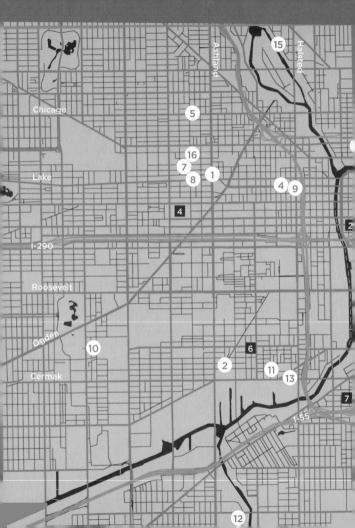

CITY NEAR LOOP

1. All Rise
2. Alulu
3. Baderbräu
4. Cruz Blanca
5. Forbidden Root
6. Gino's
7. Goose Island
8. Great Central
9. Haymarket
10. Lagunitas
11. Lo Rez
12. Marz
13. Moody Tongue
14. Motor Row
15. Off Color
16. On Tour
17. Vice District

NEIGHBORHOOD HIGHLIGHTS

1 Navy Pier
2 Willis Tower
3 Michigan Ave. Shopping
4 United Center
5 Museum Campus
6 Thalia Hall
7 Chinatown

ALL RISE BREWING CO.

FIELD NOTES

After years of running one of Chicago's largest music festivals (Riot Fest) and one of its more notorious punk bars (Cobra Lounge), Sean McKeough started a brewery. All Rise might be the first brewery in the country built alongside a punk bar. Head Brewer Tommy Nicely brews styles that are all very approachable and drinkable. Overall, All Rise is the logical extension of a hospitality project of some punks who want to make some beer they want to drink themselves.

235 N. Ashland Ave.
Chicago, IL 60607
312-226-6300
allrisebrewing.com

OWNER	DATE FOUNDED
All Rise Brewing	2014
HEAD BREWER	**RECENT AWARDS**
Tommy Nicely	WBC 2016
AVAILABILITY	**KEY EVENTS**
Chicago - very limited draft only	Motoblot (Jun)
BEST KNOWN FOR	**PUBLIC TRANSIT**
IPAs, wheat ales	'L' Green or Pink/ Ashland

20 | 300 | • | | • | • | | | • | • | • | 3.8/5

ALL RISE BREWING CO.

PRO TIPS

» One of the nicest and largest outdoor patios of any brewery within the city limits. Dog friendly on patio only.

» The Lounge hosts concerts on a regular basis, so this is your place to catch some tunes while sampling some brews (plan on the music being LOUD).

» Close enough to On Tour, Goose Island and Great Central that visiting all four in one outing is conceivable.

» Food specials Monday through Thursday. Menu is hearty pub grub with a focus on local sourcing.

» You certainly don't need to be a punk in order to enjoy All Rise, but it won't hurt if you can name a Naked Raygun album or two.

POPULAR BEERS

DATE OF VISIT:

MY RATING

NOTES:

M	Tu	W	Th	F	S	Su
11a-2a	11a-2a	11a-2a	11a-2a	11a-2a	5p-3a	closed

ALULU

FIELD NOTES

BREWPUB
ALULU
CHI, ILL

2011 S. Laflin St.
Chicago, IL 60608
312-600-9865
alulubrew.com

Alulu is the maiden project of Darren Lim, Frank Costanzo and Logan Helton. Each has drawn on their expertise and enthusiasm to create a wholly unique and idiosyncratic melange of food and beer on the near south side of the city. Despite just opening, Alulu boasts an impressive 15 beers on its draft lines already, all with names meant to evoke science fiction and fantasy genres. Helton's worldly travels have led to a love of Belgian and malt-driven ales that can exist without excessive hops.

OWNER
A collective of indie artists & brewers

HEAD BREWER
Logan Helton, Frank Costanzo, Jason James

AVAILABILITY
Brewpub only

BEST KNOWN FOR
IPAs, Belgians, Kettle Sours, lagers

DATE FOUNDED
2017

PUBLIC TRANSIT
'L' Pink/18th Street

| 30 | 75 | • | | • | | | • | | • | 3.7/5 |

ALULU

PRO TIPS

» In the future, look for barrel-aged and wild-fermented beers to make an appearance.

» Alulu boasts a fireplace for colder weather and large garage-style door to be opened during warmer weather.

» The restaurant's house beverage program include a line of in-house made sodas that can be consumed separately, or combined as a shandy into one of the house brews. Cocktails and beertails are also available.

» The food menu is eclectic and dynamic, with Darren Lim's creations ranging from house-made sausages and pierogi to mussels with frites and vegan egg rolls.

» Pair with visits to nearby Moody Tongue and Lo Rez.

DATE OF VISIT:

MY RATING
☆ ☆ ☆ ☆ ☆

NOTES:

POPULAR BEERS

| Jaunt Rotation | Halcyon Equinox | Libra Aura | Rue Envoy |

M	Tu	W	Th	F	S	Su
closed	closed	5p-2a	5p-2a	3p-2a	3p-3a	3p-2a

BADERBRÄU

FIELD NOTES

2515 S. Wabash Ave.
Chicago, IL 60616
312-890-2728
baderbrau.com

Baderbräu's journey is a winding one. Starting around the same time as Goose Island in the late 1980s, Baderbräu's Chicago Pilsner was a local favorite in the burgeoning craft beer boom of the 1990s. Over-ambition and over-expansion led to hard times for Baderbräu, whose parent company declared bankruptcy in 1997. Goose Island took up the Baderbräu mantle, brewing the famous Chicago Pilsner for a short time before Rob Sama acquired the name, recipe, and yeast strain in 2010. He's been expanding the German-inspired, lager-centric beers ever since.

OWNER Rob Sama	**DATE FOUNDED** 2012
HEAD BREWER Nathan Tertell	**KEY EVENTS** South Side Beer Fest (May)
AVAILABILITY Chicago	**PUBLIC TRANSIT** 'L' Red or Green/ Cermak-McCormick Place
BEST KNOWN FOR Lagers, American takes on German styles	

10 | 162 | | | • | • | | • | | • | 3.9/5

BADERBRÄU

PRO TIPS

» The newly-opened kitchen at the taproom features sandwiches and shareable appetizers, including something called a "Mac & Cheese Waffle" that begs to be experienced in person.

» Baderbrau's upstairs taproom is spacious with plenty of room at the bar and a number of tables to accommodate a larger group if necessary.

» They are very proud of their South Side location. They brew a beer called South Side Pride and are big fans of the Chicago White Sox.

» Their space is very popular for weddings and other private events, so call ahead to ensure they're open.

DATE OF VISIT:

MY RATING
☆ ☆ ☆ ☆ ☆

NOTES:

POPULAR BEERS

M	Tu	W	Th	F	S	Su
closed	3-11p	3-11p	3-12a	3-12a	12p-12a	3-11p

CRUZ BLANCA BREWERY + TAQUERIA

FIELD NOTES

Rick Bayless, one of the true titans of Chicago's restaurant scene, took special care and made no shortcuts when opening his first brewpub. Cruz Blanca is located in the hip West Loop neighborhood, on the stretch of Randolph Street near plenty of other notable restaurants, cocktail bars, and nightlife. Like many other Rick Bayless restaurants, the cuisine is Mexican street-food inspired, with fresh-made tacos and other Oaxacan specialties. The beers themselves are inspired by Mexican-style craft lagers and Mexican food ingredients.

904 W. Randolph St.
Chicago, IL 60607
312-733-1975
cruzblanca.com

OWNER
Manny Valdes, Rick Bayless

HEAD BREWER
Jacob Sembrano

AVAILABILITY
Brewpub only

BEST KNOWN FOR
Mexican style lagers, food infused beers

DATE FOUNDED
2016

KEY EVENTS
Anniversary Party (May), Cinco de Mayo (May), Das Bueno Oktoberfest (Sept), New Year's Eve (Dec)

PUBLIC TRANSIT
'L' Green or Pink/ Morgan

| 12 | 67 | • | • | • | | • | | • | 3.8/5 |

CRUZ BLANCA BREWERY + TAQUERIA

PRO TIPS

» Dog friendly on the patio only.

» Rated #4 new brewery in the U.S. by USA Today in 2016.

» Limited to-go bottles can sometimes be purchased on-site.

» Like many other West Loop destinations with good beer, Cruz Blanca will fill up with the post-work crowd on many weeknights after 5p, so go during afternoons or on weekends when there's no work crowd.

» If you take a seat at the bar, you can order food there; no need to stand in the food line.

» Large upstairs room with another bar is open Thursday to Sunday.

» Check out the new weekend brunch.

POPULAR BEERS

| Mexico Calling Lager | El Train IPA | Free-town Double IPA | Barba Negra Coconut Porter |

DATE OF VISIT:

MY RATING
☆ ☆ ☆ ☆ ☆

NOTES:

M	Tu	W	Th	F	S	Su
closed	11a-12a	11a-12a	11a-12a	11a-12a	10a-12a	10a-9p

FORBIDDEN ROOT

FIELD NOTES

1746 W. Chicago Ave.
Chicago, IL 60622
312-929-2202
forbiddenroot.com

Forbidden Root is a craft brewery inspired by nature. Creativity and experimentation are in the forefront, as Forbidden Root often utilizes wild ingredients and botanicals to create a variety of beers that are both familiar and eccentric, yet always flavorful. In particular, the brewery gained notoriety in 2017 for churning out an impressive collection of New England IPAs. Whatever style you choose, you can be sure there's an item on the seasonal food menu that will complement and elevate your selection.

OWNER
Robert Finkel

HEAD BREWER
Nick Williams

AVAILABILITY
Chicago, FL, OH

BEST KNOWN FOR
Spiced/herbed ales,
NE IPAs

DATE FOUNDED
2013

PUBLIC TRANSIT
'L' Blue/Division

16 | 258 | | | • | | | • | | • | 4.1/5

FORBIDDEN ROOT

PRO TIPS

» Located in the hip East Village neighborhood, enjoy the local flavor with Chicago Avenue's array of cafés, record stores, and even a true-blue western-wear outfitter.

» Furnished with couches, tables for groups and a large bar in the middle, the space is perfect for any occasion from dinner with friends, to drinks on a date, to birthday celebrations.

» 100% of their profits from non-consumable merchandise is donated to a rotating charity.

» Reservations are recommended on weekend evenings.

DATE OF VISIT:

MY RATING
☆ ☆ ☆ ☆ ☆

NOTES:

POPULAR BEERS

M	Tu	W	Th	F	S	Su
11:30-12	11:30-12	11:30-12	11:30-12	11:30-12	11a-12a	11a-10p

GINO'S BREWING CO.

FIELD NOTES

Gino's East is generally regarded as one of the main three progenitors of the Chicago-style deep dish pizza. For the uninitiated, Chicago-style deep dish is a massive, multi-layered creation that features a hearty, bready crust, a helping of cheese that would make any cardiologist or dairy farmer blush, and the tomato sauce on the top of the pie. It's a mandatory experience for the Chicago tourist. Around since 1966, Gino's East became the first of the big three Chicago pizza joints to open a brewery in one of their locations in 2015.

500 N. LaSalle Dr.
Chicago, IL 60654
312-988-4200
ginoseast.com

OWNER
Bravo Restaurants

HEAD BREWER
Kevin McMahon

AVAILABILITY
Gino's East
restaurants only

BEST KNOWN FOR
Session ales, pales

DATE FOUNDED
2015

RECENT AWARDS
U.S. Open Beer Cup
2015

PUBLIC TRANSIT
'L' Red/Grand,
Brown/Merch. Mart

11 | 340 | • | | • | • | | • | | | • | 3.6/5

GINO'S BREWING CO.

PRO TIPS

» Give yourself plenty of time at Gino's, as getting a table usually takes some patience, depending on the size of your party. Also, allow yourself time to enjoy a deep-dish pie; it goes a long way toward soaking up the beer.

» In its short history, Gino's has won an impressive number of awards, including several at the 2015 U.S. Open Beer Cup.

» The multi-level facility also features live music and a comedy club.

» Michael Jordan's Restaurant occupied the space from 1993 to 1999.

DATE OF VISIT:

MY RATING
☆ ☆ ☆ ☆ ☆

NOTES:

POPULAR BEERS

Broken English	Witte Chicks Dig Me	LaSalle Street	Pine-apple Imposter

M	Tu	W	Th	F	S	Su
11a-10p	11a-10p	11a-10p	11a-10p	11a-11p	11a-11p	11a-10p

GOOSE ISLAND BEER CO.

FIELD NOTES

1800 W. Fulton St.
Chicago, IL 60612
312-226-1119
gooseisland.com

Goose Island is, for all intents and purposes, the granddaddy of craft beer in Chicago. The longest-running brewery in Chicago, Goose Island began as a small brewpub in a then-run down industrial part of the Lincoln Park neighborhood. Founder John Hall returned from a European sojourn with a love for the continent's beer and the culture surrounding it. In 2015, Goose Island added a taproom to their production facility in the Fulton Market neighborhood. The taproom features some experimental and exclusive beers, as well as plenty of longtime favorites.

OWNER
AB InBev

HEAD BREWER
Jared Jankowski

AVAILABILITY
Nationwide

BEST KNOWN FOR
Pales, barrel-aged beers

DATE FOUNDED
1988

KEY EVENTS
BCBS Release (Nov), 312 Block Party (Sept)

PUBLIC TRANSIT
'L' Green or Pink/Ashland (Fulton)

16 | 100 | | | | | | | | • | 3.9/5

GOOSE ISLAND BEER CO.

PRO TIPS

» Visit their other location at: 1800 N. Clybourn Ave., Chicago IL (the original brewpub).

» The stylish and modern taproom has plenty of vintage bottles and Goose memorabilia for sale.

» The bar will get packed with the post-work crowd and on weekends, so retreat to one of several tables if you don't want folks shouting a beer order behind you.

» Rare beers will show up randomly on the draft list including Bourbon County Stout variants.

» The recently remodeled brewpub opens the space up considerably with modern changes to the decor that look sleek and stylish.

DATE OF VISIT:

MY RATING

NOTES:

POPULAR BEERS

M	Tu	W	Th	F	S	Su
closed	closed	2-8p	2-8p	2-9p	12-9p	12-6p

GREAT CENTRAL BREWING COMPANY

FIELD NOTES

221 N. Wood St.
Chicago, IL 60612
855-464-4222
**greatcentralbrew-
ing.com**

You often hear about breweries using contract facilities to supplement production of their own beer, whether it's for lack of brewing equipment or an excess of demand. Great Central opened primarily as a contract facility, producing beers for other breweries on their equipment. Fortunately, their Bavarian brewmaster has leeway to produce a few of their own German-style brews as well. This combination allows the taproom to feature a wide range of styles from different breweries on their 24 taps, all made under one roof.

OWNER
Private

HEAD BREWER
Andreas Miller,
Laura Berns

AVAILABILITY
Chicago

BEST KNOWN FOR
German styles

DATE FOUNDED
2017

PUBLIC TRANSIT
'L' Green or Pink/
Ashland

24 | 182 | | | • | | | | | • | 3.9/5

GREAT CENTRAL BREWING COMPANY

PRO TIPS

» The tasting room is sizeable with bar seating and a plethora of German beer hall-style tables.

» Perfect spot before a concert, Bulls or Blackhawks game at the United Center.

» Great Central is part of the Chicago Brewing District, an area where you can hit multiple taprooms (Goose, On Tour, etc.) in one visit. There's even a trolley on the weekends.

» Recent client beer that has been on tap at Great Central includes Maplewood, Begyle, Kinslahger and Pennsylvania's Funk Brewing.

» Work on your top spin while enjoying a beer on their new ping-pong table.

DATE OF VISIT:

MY RATING
☆ ☆ ☆ ☆ ☆

NOTES:

POPULAR BEERS

Hefewei-zen	Pilsner	Weizen-bock	Helles Lager

M	Tu	W	Th	F	S	Su
closed	closed	2-8p	2-9p	2-9p	12-9p	12-8p

HAYMARKET PUB & BREWERY

FIELD NOTES

737 W. Randolph St.
Chicago, IL 60661
312-638-0700
haymarketbrewing.com

Haymarket Square, on Chicago's near west side, is the site of, arguably, the birth of the American (and worldwide) labor movement. The "Haymarket Affair" was the inspiration for many of the world's May Day celebrations for workers' rights. Pete Crowley, who got his start as the head brewer at Rock Bottom Chicago, branched out with his this venture in the West Loop in 2010. Crowley's beers have won many awards over the years and while Haymarket is still one of the neighborhood landmarks, a massive culinary and hip scene has developed around it.

Gosia Photography

OWNER John Neurauter, Pete Crowley	**DATE FOUNDED** 2010
HEAD BREWER Pete Crowley	**2017 PRODUCTION** 1,200 bbl
AVAILABILITY Chicagoland, SW MI	**RECENT AWARDS** FoBAB 2017, WBC 2016
BEST KNOWN FOR IPAs, pales, Belgians	**KEY EVENTS** SausageFest (Feb)
	PUBLIC TRANSIT 'L' Green or Pink/ Clinton

24 | 400 | • | | | • | • | • | | • | | | • | 3.7/5

HAYMARKET PUB & BREWERY

PRO TIPS

» The space is sizable with a bar area and a dining room both ready to accommodate plenty.

» The back bar is a great venue for live music.

» The food menu is standard pub grub, done well. Expect sandwiches, pizzas and entrées plus a sweet potato tots appetizer that'll make you want an industrial-sized bag of them for home). Brunch on weekends.

» Haymarket runs a production facility in Bridgman, Michigan that allows Haymarket to expand distribution beyond the brewpub.

» Both bars feature plenty of TV's always tuned into the latest sporting events.

Gosia Photography

DATE OF VISIT:

MY RATING
☆ ☆ ☆ ☆ ☆

NOTES:

POPULAR BEERS

M	Tu	W	Th	F	S	Su
11a-2a	11a-2a	11a-2a	11a-2a	11a-2a	11a-3a	11a-2a

LAGUNITAS BREWING COMPANY

FIELD NOTES

Lagunitas founder Tony Magee has admittedly always been a Chicago guy, though he started the brewery in his family's home in California. After building a sizable operation in Petaluma, Lagunitas expanded to this enormous facility on the south side of Chicago near Jackson Park. Housed in an old movie studio, Lagunitas turned it into the largest brewery in the city. In fact, combine all of the other breweries in the state of Illinois and you still won't match their production capacity. This place is big!

1843 S. Washtenaw Ave.
Chicago, IL 60608
773-522-1308
lagunitas.com

OWNER Heineken	**DATE FOUNDED** 1993
HEAD BREWER Mary Bauer	**KEY EVENTS** Beer Circus (Sept)
AVAILABILITY Nationwide	**PUBLIC TRANSIT** 'L' Pink/California
BEST KNOWN FOR Everything hoppy	

16 | 250 | | | • | | | • | • | • | 4.1/5

LAGUNITAS BREWING COMPANY

PRO TIPS

» Due to the massive size of the facility, the complimentary Lagunitas brewery tour is one not to miss. In addition to free beer, you'll be taken out onto the catwalks that traverse the space, giving you a bird's eye view of the brewing, packaging and shipping operations that make a brewery of this scale hum.

» The tones of "Pure Imagination" from Willy Wonka and the Chocolate Factory will serenade you as you enter.

» A small food menu has snacks, shareables, burgers and sandwiches.

» Live music most weekends and a large Schwag Shop where you can buy any logo'd item imaginable.

DATE OF VISIT:

MY RATING
☆ ☆ ☆ ☆ ☆

NOTES:

POPULAR BEERS

M	Tu	W	Th	F	S	Su
closed	closed	12-9p	12-9p	12-9p	12-9p	12-9p

LO REZ BREWING

FIELD NOTES

2101 S. Carpenter St.
Chicago, IL 60608
888-404-2262
lorezbrewing.com

Like many other breweries before it, Lo Rez began as a garage project. The project outgrew its garage and after a few years of planning and building, Lo Rez's taproom opened in 2017 as the brainchild of Kevin Lilly and Dave Dahl. Lilly left his tech career for brewing and a Siebel degree, working at 5 Rabbit and Metropolitan before launching Lo Rez. The name of the game here is drinkable beers that go easy on the hops. While this iconoclastic, low-hop approach might seem contrarian in today's landscape, it fits in perfectly with their mantra of utilizing old world craftsmanship and beer to bring people together.

OWNER
Dave Dahl, Kevin Lilly

HEAD BREWER
Kevin Lilly

AVAILABILITY
Chicago - draft only

BEST KNOWN FOR
Belgians, malt forward beers

DATE FOUNDED
2016

KEY EVENTS
Taproom Anniversary (June)

12 | 99 | • | • | • | | • | | | 3.9/5

LO REZ BREWING

PRO TIPS

» There's a vintage feel to the taproom, exemplified by the tap menu that's written on three large reclaimed doors, and can be easily read even from a bit of a distance.

» Lo Rez's adjacent porch is the rare outdoor space that's also covered from the elements.

» Closely tied into the rich cultural hertiage of Pilsen, Lo Rez hosts an ever-changing list of bands, DJ's, poetry and art events.

» Cheese flights and artisanal jerky are available for snacks.

» Pair with a visit to the nearby Moody Tongue and Alulu.

DATE OF VISIT:

MY RATING
☆ ☆ ☆ ☆ ☆

NOTES:

POPULAR BEERS

Daemon	Primary Element	Memory Fault	Shortcut

M	Tu	W	Th	F	S	Su
closed	closed	2-10p	2-10p	2-10p	12-10p	12-8p

MARZ COMMUNITY BREWING

FIELD NOTES

3630 S. Iron St.
Chicago, IL 60609
773-579-1935
marzbrewing.com

Marz is a self-described collective of home brewers, professional brewers and artists, brought together while drinking at Maria's Packaged Goods & Community Bar in Bridgeport, and connected by a shared belief in small batch, socially responsible brewing. The taproom opened in 2018 and is a natural extension of the Southside cultural empire that includes Maria's and Kimski, a Polish-Korean street food diner. As one might expect, Marz's space is visually striking and stylish, spotlights local artists, and offers an array of inspired, experimental brews (including their popular North East IPAs).

OWNER
Ed Marszewski

HEAD BREWER
Tim Lange, Eric Olson

AVAILABILITY
Chicago, limited other markets

BEST KNOWN FOR
NE IPAs, wild sours, beer with tea

DATE FOUNDED
2014

KEY EVENTS
Level Eater (Jan), Marzivesarry (Oct)

24 | 173 | | | • | | | • | • | | | 4.1/5

MARZ COMMUNITY BREWING

PRO TIPS

» Marz is just 1.5 miles west of Guaranteed Rate Field, home of the White Sox.

» Pair with a visit to 3rd Fridays/Open Studios at the nearby Bridgeport Art Center.

» Marz' commitment local neighborhood art and culture is further evidenced by the art space adjacent to the taproom, where visitors can bring their drink and peruse the pieces.

» Chef Tony Balestreri, previously at Kimski and Fat Rice, offers unique takes on snacks, sandwiches and salads.

» Marz collaborates with and supports Lumpen Magazine, Mash Tun Journal, Lumpen Radio, and the art space Co-Prosperity Sphere.

POPULAR BEERS

DATE OF VISIT:

MY RATING
☆ ☆ ☆ ☆ ☆

NOTES:

M	Tu	W	Th	F	S	Su
closed	closed	11a-10p	11a-10p	11a-11p	12-11p	12-8p

MOODY TONGUE BREWING COMPANY

FIELD NOTES

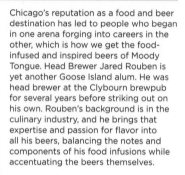

2136 S. Peoria St.
Chicago, IL 60608
312-600-5111
moodytongue.com

Chicago's reputation as a food and beer destination has led to people who began in one arena forging into careers in the other, which is how we get the food-infused and inspired beers of Moody Tongue. Head Brewer Jared Rouben is yet another Goose Island alum. He was head brewer at the Clybourn brewpub for several years before striking out on his own. Rouben's background is in the culinary industry, and he brings that expertise and passion for flavor into all his beers, balancing the notes and components of his food infusions while accentuating the beers themselves.

OWNER
Jared Rouben

HEAD BREWER
Jared Rouben

AVAILABILITY
AL, GA, IL, KY, NV, SC, TX, WI, Canada, China

BEST KNOWN FOR
IPAs, saisons, food-infused beers

DATE FOUNDED
2014

PUBLIC TRANSIT
'L' Orange/Halsted

12 | 75 | | | • | | • | | | • | | • | 4.0/5

MOODY TONGUE BREWING COMPANY

PRO TIPS

» There's no sign for Moody Tongue so you'll have to look for the unmarked door on the side of the building.

» Expect a modern, luxurious minimalism at the tasting room. This might be the most stylish brewery space in the city.

» The food menu features only two items: fresh oysters and an endlessly-layered German chocolate cake. Both are designed to pair with Rouben's "chef-driven" beer options.

» On rare occasions, guests can try small pours of the Shaved Black Truffle Pilsner made with rare mushrooms.

» Pair with visits to nearby Lo Rez and Alulu.

POPULAR BEERS

Jordan Balderas

DATE OF VISIT:

MY RATING
☆ ☆ ☆ ☆ ☆

NOTES:

M	Tu	W	Th	F	S	Su
5-10p	closed	closed	5-11p	5-12a	12p-12a	12-9p

MOTOR ROW BREWING

FIELD NOTES

2337 S. Michigan Ave.
Chicago, IL 60616
312-624-8149
**motorrowbrewing.
com**

Head Brewer Frank Lassandrello is a Goose Island alum whose travels have brought him back to Chicago and Motor Row. Motor Row is located in the historical district that unofficially shares its name with this rather new brewery. A fine balance of lagers and ales has always been Lassandrello's specialty, and he continues that at Motor Row. Scores of auto-related manufacturers and dealers used to be housed on this stretch of Michigan Avenue, which also has a deep music history as Record Row (Chess Records, Vee-Jay Records and more).

OWNER
Bob Lassandrello

HEAD BREWER
Frank Lassandrello

AVAILABILITY
Chicago

BEST KNOWN FOR
Lagers, American ales

DATE FOUNDED
2015

PUBLIC TRANSIT
'L' Red or Green/
Cermak-McCormick
Place

8 | 200 | | • | • | • | • | | • | | • | 3.9/5

MOTOR ROW BREWING

PRO TIPS

» Both growlers and canned howlers are available for purchase.

» Live blues jam every Thursday night.

» Expect to see a number of out-of-towners due to its proximity to the McCormick Place Convention Center.

» Motor Row will likely become a popular pregame destination for the Wintrust Arena, the new home of DePaul basketball for the 2017-18 season.

» If you're in the mood for food while at Motor Row, check-out the neighbors 14 Parish who will deliver to your seat for free.

DATE OF VISIT:

MY RATING
☆ ☆ ☆ ☆ ☆

NOTES:

POPULAR BEERS

Fleet-wood Black	Recla-mation Lager	New Phenix Lager	Dry Humor Begian

M	Tu	W	Th	F	S	Su
4-10p	4-10p	4-10p	4-10p	12-11p	12-11p	2-8p

OFF COLOR BREWING

FIELD NOTES

1460 N. Kingsbury St.
Chicago, IL 60642
312-929-2916
offcolorbrewing.com

Off Color's Mousetrap taproom exists in a unique locale. While Lincoln Park is one of the city's more well-to-do residential and business districts, Off Color's location in the shadows of a massive Whole Foods in a bustling corridor still feels tucked away and almost secret. Although Off Color's been producing beer since 2013, a space to sit and enjoy their brews didn't exist until October 2017. Once inside, you'll be treated to a selection of some of the most adventurous and well-crafted beers Chicago has to offer.

Jeremy Farmer

OWNER
John Laffler, Dave Bleitner

HEAD BREWER
John Laffler, Dave Bleitner

AVAILABILITY
37 states

BEST KNOWN FOR
Farmhouse ales, wild ales, historical/experimental beers, stouts

DATE FOUNDED
2013

PUBLIC TRANSIT
'L' Red/North-Clybourn

16 | 123 | • | • | • | | | | • | • | 4.1/5

OFF COLOR BREWING

PRO TIPS

- » Visit their other location at: 3925 W. Dickens, Chicago, IL (bottle shop only).
- » Dog friendly on the patio only.
- » If your personal beer tastes fall into the "IPA, all IPA, and nothing but IPA" category, then you should probably turn around and head somewhere else. Off Color's focus has been decidedly anti-hoppy since their inception and it's worked to their advantage.
- » Be sure to try the house cocktails. As with the beer, they're inspired, risk-taking and thoughtful.
- » Make this a stop before or after a visit to the iO Theater, one of Chicago's best improv comedy spots.

Jeremy Farmer

DATE OF VISIT:

MY RATING
☆ ☆ ☆ ☆ ☆

NOTES:

POPULAR BEERS

M	Tu	W	Th	F	S	Su
11a-11p	11a-11p	11a-11p	11a-11p	11a-12a	11a-12a	11a-11p

ON TOUR BREWING CO.

FIELD NOTES

1725 W. Hubbard St.
Chicago, IL 60622
312-796-3119
**ontourbrewingco.
com**

Newly opened in January 2017, On Tour is the brainchild of Mark Legenza. He started homebrewing in Denver in 2009 and moved back to Chicago in 2015 to open the music-themed On Tour. Not only the Founder/Owner, Mark assumed brewing responsibilities in January 2018. Of note, after being open for only nine short months, On Tour shocked the craft brewing world by not only winning two medals at the 2017 Great American Beer Festival, but also took home the prize for top Very Small Brewing Company. A huge feat for such a young brewery.

Amanda Campagnoni

OWNER Mark Legenza	**DATE FOUNDED** 2017
HEAD BREWER Mark Legenza	**2017 PRODUCTION** 735
AVAILABILITY Chicago - limited draft only	**RECENT AWARDS** GABF 2017 (3)
BEST KNOWN FOR IPAs, pilsners, sours	**PUBLIC TRANSIT** 'L' Green/Ashland

12 | 98 | | | • | • | | | • | 4.1/5

ON TOUR BREWING CO.

PRO TIPS

» Focuses on brewing a variety of "approachable" beers for people to take a moment to "press pause and enjoy."

» GABF winnings included gold medal for their Maibock, Low Boy, and silver medal for their Doppelbock, Spectator.

» On Tour hosts a variety of food trucks and pop-ups in their tasting room. Past trucks and pop-up include Porkchop, Cheesies and Arigato Tacos.

» Not far from United Center in case you want to catch a Blackhawks or Bulls game.

» The space is bright and vibrant with a big opening behind the bar providing a direct view into the brewhouse.

» Credit card only.

POPULAR BEERS

It Takes Two	Light-ning Will	Silly Grin	Specta-tor

M	Tu	W	Th	F	S	Su
3-10p	3-10p	3-10p	3-10p	2-11p	11a-11p	11a-8p

Vanessa Buholzer

DATE OF VISIT:

MY RATING
☆ ☆ ☆ ☆ ☆

NOTES:

VICE DISTRICT BREWING CO.

FIELD NOTES

1454 S. Michigan Ave.
Chicago, IL 60605
312-291-9022
**vicedistrictbrewing.
com**

South Side Chicago natives Quintin Cole and Curtis Tarver II unknowingly put themselves on the road to starting Vice District Brewing when they bought homes across the street from one another. In what sounds like a sitcom plot, the two were soon homebrewing together, hosting beer gatherings, and ultimately deciding to start their own venture in the South Loop neighborhood. Cole and Tarver's plan is to be that gathering place where people can enter as guests but leave as friends.

OWNER
Curtis Tarver II,
Quintin Cole

HEAD BREWER
Aydan Connor

AVAILABILITY
Taproom only

BEST KNOWN FOR
IPAs, American takes on English styles

DATE FOUNDED
2013

PUBLIC TRANSIT
'L' Red, Green or Orange/Roosevelt

16 | 99 | | • | • | • | | | | • | 3.8/5

VICE DISTRICT BREWING CO.

PRO TIPS

» Lots of bar seating and beer-hall style tables, with windows that open wide on warm days.

» Beers are British-inspired for the most part, with some Belgian and German interjections.

» Regularly hosted events seem to have a fitness theme. Wednesdays are the meetings of the Vice District Run Club and every other Saturday afternoon features body workout classes like Pure Barre or Vinyasa. Check their website calendar for details.

» A second location with a production facility and taproom is currently in the works for downtown Homewood, IL in the south suburbs.

» Board games are available.

DATE OF VISIT:

MY RATING
☆ ☆ ☆ ☆ ☆

NOTES:

POPULAR BEERS

Habitual Pleasure Trip Everleigh

M	Tu	W	Th	F	S	Su
closed	4-11p	4-11p	4-11p	4p-1a	2p-1a	2-9p

CITY SOUTH

1 Horse Thief Hollow
2 Open Outcry
3 Whiner

NEIGHBORHOOD HIGHLIGHTS

1 Guaranteed Rate
   Field

2 The Pullman State
   Historic Site

3 The Original
   Rainbow Cone

HORSE THIEF HOLLOW BREWING CO.

FIELD NOTES

10426 S. Western Ave.
Chicago, IL 60643
773-779-2739
**horsethiefbrewing.
com**

Located on the far south side in the Beverly neighborhood, Horse Thief Hollow is well worth the time to get there. In a space that used to be occupied by a carpet store, Horse Thief Hollow has established itself as a vital cultural outpost for the community. After working for almost a decade as a chef in Charleston, SC, Neil Byers enlisted help from his entire family in renovating Horse Thief Hollow's current space, even using reclaimed carved-wood doors for the building's entrance. The beers and food are given just as much care as their surroundings.

OWNER
Neil Byers

HEAD BREWER
David Williams

AVAILABILITY
Chicago - limited

BEST KNOWN FOR
Pales, IPAs, stouts,
Kölsch

DATE FOUNDED
2013

2017 PRODUCTION
580 bbl

RECENT AWARDS
GABF 2016, 2017,
FoBAB 2016

PUBLIC TRANSIT
RI/103rd St.-Beverly
Hills

12 | 160 | | | • | • | | • | • | • | 3.8/5

HORSE THIEF HOLLOW BREWING CO.

PRO TIPS

» The food menu, as Byers' history might indicate, is "Southern gastropub" inspired with BBQ, Gumbo, Illinois raised Lamb Burgers and house made sausages.

» Monthly live music shows and Art on Tap, a series showcasing the work of local artists.

» Chicago Magazine named it one of the top 50 bars in Chicago.

» If you make the trip to Horse Thief Hollow, you must also visit the legendary Original Rainbow Cone (in season).

» Make your trip a double stop with Open Outcry Brewing Co. which is less than a mile south.

DATE OF VISIT:

MY RATING
☆ ☆ ☆ ☆ ☆

NOTES:

POPULAR BEERS

Parallel Universe NEIPA	Kitchen Sink Pale Ale	Ridge Rider	18th Re-bellion

M	Tu	W	Th	F	S	Su
11.30-10	11.30-10	11.30-10	11.30-10	11.30-12	11.30-12	11.30-10

OPEN OUTCRY BREWING

FIELD NOTES

10934 S. Western Ave.
Chicago, IL 60643
773-629-6055
openoutcrybrewing.com

Morgan Park is one of the city's southernmost neighborhoods, and as a result, it sometimes gets overlooked with respect to Chicago neighborhood exploration. But there are plenty of wonderful spots to visit, especially for craft beer fans now that Open Outcry has opened just down the road from Horse Thief Hollow. Open Outcry offers guests a friendly, welcoming space with a nice mix of sessionable, easy-drinking beers for the masses, as well as challenging, complex ales for the craft connoisseur. Plus, an indoor "food truck" (you'll understand when you visit).

OWNER
John Brand

HEAD BREWER
John Brand, Will Golebiewski

AVAILABILITY
Brewpub only

BEST KNOWN FOR
IPAs, NE IPAs, imperial stouts, cream ale

DATE FOUNDED
2017

PUBLIC TRANSIT
RI/111th St.

| 17 | 115 | | | • | • | | • | • | | 4.1/5 |

OPEN OUTCRY BREWING

PRO TIPS

» The distressed woodwork on Open Outcry's exterior looks smart and stylish as you travel down Western Avenue. With Edison bulbs and other modern architectural choices, you'd never know the space was the former home of O'Brien's Irish Pub.

» One of the few spots in town where you can get a beer poured directly from one of the tanks.

» While there's no formal outdoor seating, the garage-style windows can be thrown open during warm weather to make you feel like you're outside.

» Make your visit to this side of town count with stops at the Beverly Art Center and Original Rainbow Cone.

DATE OF VISIT:

MY RATING
☆ ☆ ☆ ☆ ☆

NOTES:

POPULAR BEERS

Open Interest	Louis Winthorpe	Speculator	Black-Scholes

M	Tu	W	Th	F	S	Su
11a-11p	11a-11p	11a-11p	11a-11p	11a-11p	11a-11p	11a-11p

WHINER BEER CO.

FIELD NOTES

WHINER BEER CO

1400 W. 46th St.
Chicago, IL 60609
312-810-2271
whinerbeer.com

Whiner is, like a few Chicago breweries, a bit of a refreshing anomaly. There are no IPA's and the taproom isn't located in a heavily-trafficked neighborhood. That said, head brewer Brian Taylor, a Goose Island alum, is brewing an impressive array of wild and barrel-aged beers while Ria Neri, who's developed beer programs for several Chicago restaurants, is focusing on the business side. The beers all have a hint of sourness to them, but that doesn't mean they're unapproachable.

OWNER
Brian Taylor, Ria Neri

DATE FOUNDED
2016

HEAD BREWER
Brian Taylor

AVAILABILITY
Chicago

BEST KNOWN FOR
Sours, lighter Belgians

| 10 | 100 | | | • | | • | | | | • | | 4.2/5 |

WHINER BEER CO.

PRO TIPS

» Whiner is located in The Plant, a unique sustainable business project with a fish farm, farmers' market and other businesses designed to use each other's resources to create a net-zero energy facility. There's nothing else like it in the city.

» Barrel-aged beers are sometimes available in bottles to go.

» There are no bum picks on the growing tap list, including a number of Belgian and French-inspired ales with an accent on adjuncts.

» Tours of The Plant are available. Book ahead on their website.

» Expect a larger crowd on first Saturday of every month when there's a Farmers Market at The Plant from 11a-3p.

POPULAR BEERS

DATE OF VISIT:

MY RATING
☆☆☆☆☆

NOTES:

M	Tu	W	Th	F	S	Su
closed	closed	closed	2-10p	2-10p	11a-10p	1-8p

SUBURBS NORTH

NEIGHBORHOOD HIGHLIGHTS

HALF DAY BREWING

FIELD NOTES

200 Village Green
Lincolnshire, IL
60069
847-821-6933
halfdaybrewing.com

Half Day is named after the Chief of the Potawatomi tribe that helped non-native Americans first settle in the area. Right off the highway, this Native American themed brewpub offers something for everyone. The brewpub is very large, able to accommodate groups of just about any size. In the summer, they also have a large patio that allows for soaking up the sun while drinking. Note that only a few of the 40 taps are dedicated to their own beer, but they also offer a full bar, wide guest beer selection and a full menu for your hunger needs.

OWNER
Scott Ward, Mark Zych

HEAD BREWER
Brandon Boshers

AVAILABILITY
Chicago - Northern Suburbs

BEST KNOWN FOR
IPAs, dark ales

DATE FOUNDED
2015

2017 PRODUCTION
500 bbl

40 | 400 | • | | • | • | | • | • | | 3.5/5

HALF DAY BREWING

PRO TIPS

» TVs dot just about every wall, making this the perfect place to watch your favorite sports teams.

» Chicken wings are award-winning.

» Cozy up to the fireplace during Chicago's long winter months.

» It can get a bit loud around the bar area, but other dining areas do offer a softer tone.

» The patio option is second to none with cozy fire pits.

» The weekend brunch is very popular.

» Can host private events for up to 400 people.

DATE OF VISIT:

MY RATING
☆ ☆ ☆ ☆ ☆

NOTES:

POPULAR BEERS

M	Tu	W	Th	F	S	Su
11a-12a	11a-12a	11a-12a	11a-12a	11a-1a	11a-1a	11a-10p

KINGS & CONVICTS BREWING CO.

FIELD NOTES

523 Bank Lane
Highwood, IL
60040
224-707-0117
**kingsandconvicts.
com**

Highwood, IL is a minuscule suburb in the North Shore area. Its claim to fame is that it was once called "one of the toughest towns in America" by Teddy Roosevelt as he passed through on a presidential campaign. The town once hosted a large number of taverns back when nearby Fort Sheridan was a major domestic military outpost. Kings and Convicts enter Highwood as its first brewery of the craft beer boom, fronted by Englishman Chris Bradley and Aussie Brendan Watters (titular King and Convict of the brewery's name). Their beers are mainly Americanized takes on Commonwealth and European classics.

OWNER
Chris Bradley,
Brendan Watters

HEAD BREWER
Chris Bradley

AVAILABILITY
Chicago

BEST KNOWN FOR
British-style pales
and IPAs, pilsners

DATE FOUNDED
2017

2017 PRODUCTION
300 bbl

PUBLIC TRANSIT
UP-N/Highwood

8 | 30 | • | • | • | | | | • | | 4.0/5

KINGS & CONVICTS BREWING CO.

PRO TIPS

» The taproom is very small and intimate, but a large patio area adds seating and is great for summer.

» There's no actual bar seating as the entire counter is for ordering only.

» Board games are scattered around the tables for those who need something more than beer to pass the time.

» The background Motown and classic rock music doesn't interfere with conversation between tables.

» Lack auto transportation? No worries as this taproom is steps from the Highwood Metra station.

» Their most popular beers tend towards a malt forward balance, versus enamel peeling hop notes.

» Pre-filled crowler to-go cans available.

POPULAR BEERS

DATE OF VISIT:

MY RATING
☆ ☆ ☆ ☆ ☆

NOTES:

M	Tu	W	Th	F	S	Su
closed	5-10p	5-10p	5-10p	4-11p	12-11p	12-8p

LAKE BLUFF BREWING CO.

FIELD NOTES

16 E. Scranton Ave.
Lake Bluff, IL 60044
224-544-5179
lbbrew.com

In 2010, the very charming Village of Lake Bluff on Chicago's North Shore finally got its own brewery. It sits on a quaint village shopping area across the street from a wooded park, perfect for sidewalk sipping during the summer months. Lake Bluff organizes their beer menu in order of intensity, allowing pour sizes of 4, 10 and 16 ounces. While exploring their wide variety of beer, make sure to enjoy the local art carefully displayed throughout the newly remodeled space.

OWNER
Mike Dorneker

HEAD BREWER
Mike Dorneker

AVAILABILITY
Chicago - Draft only

BEST KNOWN FOR
Imperial stouts,
blonde ales, IPAs

DATE FOUNDED
2010

RECENT AWARDS
FoBAB 2016

PUBLIC TRANSIT
UP-N/Lake Bluff

| 14 | 60 | • | • | • | | | | ℗ | | • | 3.8/5 |

LAKE BLUFF BREWING CO.

PRO TIPS

» Dog friendly on the patio only.

» While food is not prepared on site, you can easily order food from the Maevery Public House next door and have it delivered right to your table.

» Hope to soon be distributing beyond just draft to the local market.

» Watch for great summer block parties.

» The Metra drops you off only steps from the brewery's front door.

» Load up your bikes and take advantage of the numerous bike trails around this tranquil community.

» Frequent live music and great rotating selection of artwork from local artists and beyond.

DATE OF VISIT:

MY RATING
☆ ☆ ☆ ☆ ☆

NOTES:

POPULAR BEERS

Inspiration Pale Ale	Skull And Bones	Velvet Hammer Vanilla Porter	Honey Badger

M	Tu	W	Th	F	S	Su
closed	5-10p	5-10p	3-11p	11:30-12	11:30-12	11:30-8

MACUSHLA BREWING

FIELD NOTES

1516 E. Lake Ave.
Glenview, IL 60025
847-730-5199
macushlabeer.com

You won't find many breweries with a more interesting family history than Mike and Megan Welch of Macushla. Mike's grandfather, Jim, used to update the odds in the gambling house in the basement of Gigi's Closette, the bridal boutique next to Macushla. "Chalk Eater", their flagship IPA, is a reference to what Jim would have to do if the gambling house was raided. Macushla Brewery is adjacent to Hackney's on Lake, the long-running burger restaurant run by Mike's family members.

OWNER
Mike Welch, Megan Welch

HEAD BREWER
Eric Plata

AVAILABILITY
Draft only - north suburbs

BEST KNOWN FOR
IPAs, NE IPAs, stouts

DATE FOUNDED
2017

PUBLIC TRANSIT
MD-N/Glenview

| 12 | 34 | • | • | • | • | | • | • | • | 4.1/5 |

MACUSHLA BREWING

PRO TIPS

» Dog friendly on the patio only.

» "Macushla" is a bastardization of the Irish language phrase "mo chuisle", which literally means "my pulse", or, more informally, "my darling" (the same phrase is also featured in the Hilary Swank-Clint Eastwood film Million Dollar Baby).

» The bar itself is small with only 34 seats so get there early on the weekends to grab a spot outside in the larger, outdoor beer garden. The feel of the taproom is understandably cozy, but not cramped.

» While there's technically no kitchen, you have easy access to the full menu at Hackney's next door.

DATE OF VISIT:

MY RATING

NOTES:

POPULAR BEERS

Chalk Eater	Loumi- nator	Kitz	Sans Souci

M	Tu	W	Th	F	S	Su
closed	12-11p	12-11p	12-11p	12p-1a	12p-1a	12-8p

MICKEY FINN'S BREWERY

FIELD NOTES

Mickey Finn's has been around since 1993 as a brewery, and as a restaurant for even longer than that (oldest brewpub in IL). Operating out of the northern suburb of Libertyville, Finn's caters to its fans, as well as its surrounding suburban audience, by hitting the middle ground between heavy and lighter styles. For every Orange Is the New Chocolate barrel-aged orange zest and chocolate stout, there's an 847 Suburban Wheat Ale (a mild dig, no doubt, at a certain Chicago brewery's Urban Wheat Ale).

345 N. Milwaukee Ave.
Libertyville, IL 60048
847-362-6688
**mickeyfinnsbrewery.
com**

OWNER
Brian Grano, Jetta Grano

HEAD BREWER
Greg Browne

AVAILABILITY
Brewpub only

BEST KNOWN FOR
IPAs, classic American styles

DATE FOUNDED
1993

KEY EVENTS
St. Paddy's Day (Mar), Get Lit (Nov)

PUBLIC TRANSIT
MD-N/Libertyville

16 | 300 | • | | • | • | • | | • | • | | • | 3.6/5

MICKEY FINN'S BREWERY

PRO TIPS

» The exposed brick and thoughtful lighting of the interior give a modern look to a business that's been around for a couple decades.

» There's a long bar offering decent seating and lots of TVs for sports watching.

» The food menu is fairly standard suburban pub fare (pizzas, burgers, spinach and artichoke dip, etc.).

» 2-for-1 burgers every Wednesday and a $4 pint of the day every Thursday.

» Live music is a feature on weekends, ranging from country to blues, but check in advance to see who is playing.

DATE OF VISIT:

MY RATING

NOTES:

POPULAR BEERS

Pine-apple Express	Santa's Magic	Amber Ale	Hefe Weizen

M	Tu	W	Th	F	S	Su
11-11:30	11-11:30	11-11:30	11-11:30	11a-1:15	11a-1:15	11a-9p

ONLY CHILD BREWING

FIELD NOTES

Ben and Amanda Rossi are the husband and wife team behind Only Child, situated near the Wisconsin border. Originally based out of Northbrook, Only Child's move to Gurnee offers the Rossi's an expansion in production, as well as taproom space. Like many other smaller operations dotting the suburban Chicago brewing landscape, the charm in Only Child is their ability to create a brewery and taproom out of what would otherwise be a lifeless industrial concrete space, injecting it with a passion and determination found in their creations.

1350 Tri State Pkwy
Gurnee, IL 60031
224-656-5241
onlychildbrewing.com

OWNER
Benjamin Rossi,
Amanda Rossi

HEAD BREWER
Benjamin Rossi

AVAILABILITY
Chicago - mostly
Lake County

BEST KNOWN FOR
IPAs, saisons

DATE FOUNDED
2013

KEY EVENTS
Anniversary
Celebration (Aug)

8 | 50 | • | • | • | • | • | | • | | 4.0/5

ONLY CHILD BREWING

PRO TIPS

» The space is rather narrow and long, so what the Only Child folks have done is split the tasting room space in two by placing the bar in the middle, essentially creating separate spaces, one closer to the door with tables, and the other closer to the brewery with barrels.

» Package releases are periodical and tend to oscillate between cans and bottles, and are sometimes cash only. Releases always sell out, so plan accordingly.

» A popular spot for special events like yoga, art fairs, monthly beer-food pairings, homebrew competitions and live music every weekend.

» Gurnee is also home to Six Flags Great America.

POPULAR BEERS

DATE OF VISIT:

MY RATING
☆ ☆ ☆ ☆ ☆

NOTES:

M	Tu	W	Th	F	S	Su
4-10p	4-10p	4-10p	4-10p	11a-11p	11a-11p	12-7p

PECKISH PIG

FIELD NOTES

Advertising itself as Evanston's first brewpub (which is true, since Temperance and Sketchbook don't have their own kitchens), Peckish Pig opened up just on the other side of the Chicago border in 2014. The space was previously used to house a dry cleaner, a nail salon, and a record store (a nice revitalization of the street). Owner Debbie Evans is originally from Liverpool and has made Peckish Pig quite the family affair, with children India and Janek both getting into the act, as well.

623 Howard St.
Evanston, IL 60202
847-491-6778
thepeckishpig.com

OWNER
Debbie Evans

HEAD BREWER
Jim Koblish,
Jonathon Armour

AVAILABILITY
Brewpub only

BEST KNOWN FOR
IPAs, Belgians,
British styles

DATE FOUNDED
2014

PUBLIC TRANSIT
'L' Red, Purple or
Yellow/Howard

12 | 180 | • | | • | • | | • | | • | 3.9/5

PECKISH PIG

PRO TIPS

- » There's a decent-sized wine list, a small cocktail list, guest beers and well-curated whiskey list.
- » Peckish Pig has a large, stylish patio available during the summer months.
- » The food menu is hearty, British-style pub fare - lamb burgers, duck confit mac n cheese, and fish & chips.
- » The bacon-wrapped dates are to die for.
- » Note that on weekends, the kitchen closes from 3:30p-4:30p to allow for the switch from brunch to dinner service.
- » Trivia nights on Tuesdays and old school dance parties every month.

POPULAR BEERS

Gin N Juice IPA	Guerilla Radio APA	Aging Hipster Amber	Benton Harbor Sour Cherry

DATE OF VISIT:

MY RATING
☆ ☆ ☆ ☆ ☆

NOTES:

M	Tu	W	Th	F	S	Su
closed	4-10p	4-10p	4-10p	4-12a	11a-12a	11a-10p

PRAIRIE KRAFTS BREWING COMPANY

FIELD NOTES

1310 Busch Pkwy
Buffalo Grove, IL
60089
224-434-2189
prairiekrafts.com

Mannish Khosla founded Prairie Krafts in order to bring craft beer to the northwestern suburb of Buffalo Grove. Khosla and co-owner Raj Chauhan provide a friendly, neighborhood vibe to the town's first brewery, offering plenty of gateway beers, and a couple of heavy hitters for those willing to jump into the deep end of the pool. Prairie Krafts does not currently package beers, but drafts are available all over the northern suburbs, and some kegs are even creeping their way into the city if you want to look hard enough.

OWNER
Mannish Khosla, Raj Chauhan

HEAD BREWER
Matt Lakota, Mannish Khosla, Raj Chauhan

AVAILABILITY
Chicago - draft only

BEST KNOWN FOR
Variety

DATE FOUNDED
2016

KEY EVENTS
Anniversary Party (Apr)

PUBLIC TRANSIT
NCS/Buffalo Grove

| 12 | 55 | | • | | • | | • | | | | • | 4.0/5 |

PRAIRIE KRAFTS BREWING COMPANY

PRO TIPS

» Prairie Krafts is located in an unassuming industrial park in the suburbs of Chicago. You will most likely drive by it your first time.

» Food trucks will only come by occasionally, so plan your eating schedule accordingly. That said, cookies made with spent grain from the brewery make frequent appearances. Try the spicy peanuts.

» Live music will be around every now and then, and even some open mic nights if you feel like bringing your own instrument.

» Features its own Mug Club for frequent customers.

DATE OF VISIT:

MY RATING
☆ ☆ ☆ ☆ ☆

NOTES:

POPULAR BEERS

M	Tu	W	Th	F	S	Su
4-9p	4-9p	4-9p	4-9p	2-11p	2-11p	2-7p

SKETCHBOOK BREWING COMPANY

FIELD NOTES

821 Chicago Ave.
Evanston, IL 60202
847-584-2337
**sketchbookbrewing.
com**

Clark Street in Chicago becomes Chicago Avenue in Evanston, and about a mile north of the border, right off the Main Street train stop is Sketchbook Brewing. Sketchbook is a tiny space that packs a lot of character into its small taproom. Much of the wood in the taproom is re-purposed, from the slats that cover the walls, to the re-purposed bowling alleys that cover the tables and bar top. Local artists also provide the neon lights and door murals on display. You can get the feeling that you're in a sort of modern day, craft beer speakeasy.

OWNER
Shawn Decker,
Cesar Marron,
Alice George, Amy
Wilkinson

HEAD BREWER
Cesar Marron

AVAILABILITY
IL

BEST KNOWN FOR
NE IPAs, pilsners,
saisons, porters,
stouts

DATE FOUNDED
2014

2017 PRODUCTION
1,450 bbl

KEY EVENTS
Anniversary Party
(Apr), Custer Fair
(Jun)

PUBLIC TRANSIT
'L' Purple/Main,
UP-N/Main

12 | 45 | | | • | | | | | • | 4.0/5

SKETCHBOOK BREWING COMPANY

PRO TIPS

» Bring your own food, no kitchen. Packaged bar snacks are available.

» Cans and growlers to go are regularly available.

» Features a CSB (community-supported brewery) program that features 1-2 regular growler fills for 6- or 12-month periods, other discounts, and invites to special events.

» Unique Lazy Lunch Happy Hour is Tuesday to Thursday from 12-3p for you early afternoon drinkers. $5 pints.

» Located in Evanston, a walk around the lively and eclectic Main-Dempster Mile neighborhood is a great activity after you're done drinking.

» Recently added more space for special event rentals.

POPULAR BEERS

ORANGE DOOR

INSUFFICIENT CLEARANCE

NIGHT GAME

Turbulence

DATE OF VISIT:

MY RATING
☆ ☆ ☆ ☆ ☆

NOTES:

M	Tu	W	Th	F	S	Su
closed	12-10p	12-10p	12-10p	12-11p	12-11p	12-8p

SMYLIE BROTHERS BREWING CO.

FIELD NOTES

SMYLIE
— brothers —
BREWING Co

1615 Oak St.
Evanston, IL 60201
224-999-7320
smyliebros.com

Owner and founder Mike Smylie went from commodities trading to the culinary world to founding this charming brewpub just north of the city of Chicago in Evanston. Smylie Brothers marries Texas-style BBQ with well-considered house-made beers. Pizza and sandwiches are also available on the food front. The main dining area features two decent-sized bars, plenty of 4-top tables, and a few booths for families. Dutch-style bikes adorn the wall above the larger of the two bars and you can get a peek at the brewing setup itself from about any seat.

OWNER Smylie Family	**DATE FOUNDED** 2014
HEAD BREWER Brad Pulver	**2017 PRODUCTION** 1,300 bbl
AVAILABILITY Brewpub and limited local draft	**RECENT AWARDS** GABF 2015, 2017 FoBAB 2016
BEST KNOWN FOR CA Common, saisons, German wheats	**PUBLIC TRANSIT** 'L' Purple/Davis, UP-N/Davis

16 | 290 | • | • | • | • | | • | | • | 3.6/5

SMYLIE BROTHERS BREWING CO.

PRO TIPS

» Dog friendly on the patio only.

» Upstairs mezzanine level features leather chairs, a fireplace and a lounge sort of atmosphere.

» Reservations are not only available for seating, but also available for indoor parking two blocks away through ParqEx (use SMYLIE promo code).

» Happy hour Tuesday to Thursday and Sunday from 4-6p. There are several drink and food specials to choose from.

» Expect to see their beer in more accounts on Chicago's North Shore soon.

DATE OF VISIT:

MY RATING
☆ ☆ ☆ ☆ ☆

NOTES:

POPULAR BEERS

Smylie Farm-house	Cali Common	Purple Line	Helles Lager

M	Tu	W	Th	F	S	Su
closed	11-10.30	11-10.30	11-10.30	11-10.30	11-11.30	11-10.30

TEMPERANCE BEER CO.

FIELD NOTES

2000 Dempster St.
Evanston, IL 60202
847-864-1000
temperancebeer.com

Evanston used to be a primary location for the Women's Christian Temperance Union, one of the largest lobbying groups that led the temperance movement in the early 1900's. Even after the repeal of prohibition in 1933, the WCTU still maintains its headquarters in Evanston. Evanston itself was dry until 1972, so shouting out the city's unique history with booze was an easy choice for the city's first brewery. Temperance features English and Belgian-inspired ales that provide unique twists on the classics.

Genie Lemieux

OWNER Josh Gilbert	**DATE FOUNDED** 2013
HEAD BREWER Dave Gibbons, Mike VanCamp	**2017 PRODUCTION** 3,300 bbl
AVAILABILITY Chicago	**RECENT AWARDS** GABF 2016
BEST KNOWN FOR Variety of complex but balanced beers	**KEY EVENTS** Greenwood Beach Day (May), Might Meets Right Release (Winter)

16 | 300 | • | | • | | • | | • | | 4.1/5

TEMPERANCE BEER CO.

PRO TIPS

» Temperance is a great place to visit during warm weather. The large garage-style door on the front of the taproom will open up to the outside and let plenty of breeze and sunshine in. Patio seating is also available.

» Play some table shuffleboard; usually gets occupied quickly.

» Yoga on the third Saturday of the month at 1p. DJ events on Fridays during the summer.

» Food trucks featured on Fridays and Sundays. Bar snacks and cheese plates are also available.

» Kid-friendly until 8p.

DATE OF VISIT:

MY RATING
☆ ☆ ☆ ☆ ☆

NOTES:

POPULAR BEERS

M	Tu	W	Th	F	S	Su
4-10p	4-10p	4-10p	4-10p	4-11p	12-11p	12-9p

TEN NINETY

FIELD NOTES

1025 Waukegan Rd.
Glenview, IL 60025
224-432-5472
ten-ninety.com

Originally this suburban brewery only featured super-big, imperial-style beers. In fact their name, Ten Ninety, refers to the high original gravity (fermentable sugar concentration) of many of their original recipes. Soon after their launch, though, Ten Ninety began branching out into lower-ABV creations. Andy and Jamie are the main men behind Ten Ninety, all having jettisoned from their jobs requiring far more advanced degrees. They originally brewed out of the Wisconsin border town of Zion, IL, before settling into their current home in Glenview, far closer to Chicago proper.

OWNER
Brian Schafer, Jamie Hoban

HEAD BREWER
Gibbs Lippai

AVAILABILITY
Chicago

BEST KNOWN FOR
Imperial ales, IPAs, witbiers

DATE FOUNDED
2013

PUBLIC TRANSIT
MD-N/Glenview

20 | 91 | • | • | • | • | | | • | • | 3.7/5

TEN NINETY

PRO TIPS

» Dog friendly on the patio only.

» Expect Ten Ninety's hours to expand when they finish adding a kitchen and upscale pub food to the taproom.

» The outside looks like a well-kept British-style pub, while the inside features a fireplace, overstuffed chairs, and a large, resplendent bar with friendly and educated staff.

» There is ample bike parking and outdoor seating for days with nicer weather.

» They occasionally have live music.

» Most of their taps are dedicated to beer that isn't distributed or available anywhere else.

DATE OF VISIT:

MY RATING
☆ ☆ ☆ ☆ ☆

NOTES:

POPULAR BEERS

M	Tu	W	Th	F	S	Su
closed	closed	4-10p	4-10p	4-10p	12-10p	12-8p

UNE ANNÉE / HUBBARD'S CAVE

FIELD NOTES

UNE ANNÉE

9082 W. Golf Rd.
Niles, IL 60714
847-635-0655
uneannee.com

Jerry Nelson's passion for brewing began while in the Marines in 1995. He attended the Siebel Institute, and, after leaving the architecture profession, started up the blueprints for what became Une Année (French for "one year") in 2013. After brewing for a couple years near Goose Island Fulton on the near west side of Chicago, Nelson found a more suitable space in the northwest suburb of Niles. Nelson spearheads both the Une Année line of French and Belgian-inspired ales, and the Hubbard's Cave brand of super-fresh IPAs and flavor-infused stouts.

OWNER
Jerry Nelson

HEAD BREWER
Jerry Nelson

AVAILABILITY
Chicagoland and limited in WI, PA, MA, GA, FL, IA, MN

BEST KNOWN FOR
Belgians, sours, Imperial IPAs

DATE FOUNDED
2013

KEY EVENTS
Monthly member-only releases

12 | 45 | • | • | • | • | • | • | • | 4.2/5

UNE ANNÉE / HUBBARD'S CAVE

PRO TIPS

» Credit card only.

» The signage out front simply states "BREWERY," barely doing justice to the biological alchemy happening inside.

» The 24-hour Omega diner and bakery is in the same complex in a stand-alone space, and is a lovely little slice of Americana for the peckish insomniac.

» Le Grand Monde is not just a series of taproom beers, but also Une Année's CSA-inspired program. Allows subscribers to prepay to reserve bottles of Nelson's experimental barrel-aged sour beers, plus bottles of a couple other beers, a taproom discount, and a t-shirt.

DATE OF VISIT:

MY RATING
☆ ☆ ☆ ☆ ☆

NOTES:

POPULAR BEERS

M	Tu	W	Th	F	S	Su
4-8p	closed	closed	2-10p	2-10p	12-10p	12-8p

ZÜMBIER

FIELD NOTES

ZümBier has been brewing out of the North Shore suburb of Waukegan since 2012, where it's been the labor of love of founder Larry Bloom and his wife Talea. Bloom's journey to craft beer began when the former whiskey drinker was handed a homebrew from his brother. That homebrew, a black rye double IPA, later become ZümBier's own Unda Cova Brudda. That moment of inspiration led Larry and Talea to pursue the idea of opening their own operation, which has culminated in ZümBier.

3232 W. Monroe St.
Waukegan, IL 60085
847-420-7313
zumbier.com

OWNER
Larry Bloom, Talea Bloom

HEAD BREWER
Larry Bloom

AVAILABILITY
Near Waukegan

BEST KNOWN FOR
Pales, IPAs, stouts, imperial styles

DATE FOUNDED
2012

KEY EVENTS
Maui Trickster Release (Spring)

13 | 30 | • | • | • | • | | | • | | 4.2/5

ZÜMBIER

PRO TIPS

» ZümBier is housed in a large aquamarine-colored building that would be hard to mistake, even from a great distance.

» Lauren, a barrel-aged imperial porter, is not the only beer worthy of a marquee bottle release. Maui Trickster, a chocolate coconut milk stout with several variants, recently saw lots of attention for its first release party.

» The taproom itself is small, with a few barstools, tables and booths.

» They still brew on a 1.5 barrel system, so one-off beers can vanish quickly. But expect these guys to grow; they have plenty of room for expansion.

» Trivia on Thursday nights at 6:30p.

DATE OF VISIT:

MY RATING
☆ ☆ ☆ ☆ ☆

NOTES:

POPULAR BEERS

Citra-Tasm	Lauren	Maui Trickster	Super Chong

M	Tu	W	Th	F	S	Su
closed	closed	4-9p	4-9p	3-10p	2-10p	1-6p

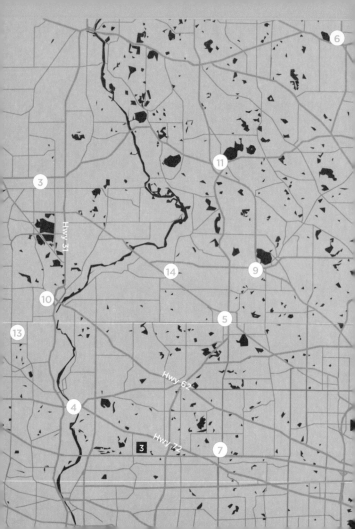

SUBURBS NORTHWEST

1. Bosacki's
2. Buffalo Creek
3. Crystal Lake
4. Emmett's
5. Flesk
6. Light The Lamp
7. The Lucky Monk
8. Mikerphone
9. Roaring Table
10. Scorched Earth
11. Side Lot
12. Tighthead
13. Village Vintner
14. Wild Onion

NEIGHBORHOOD HIGHLIGHTS

1 O'Hare Int'l Airport
2 Arlington Int'l Racecourse
3 Sears Centre Arena
4 Independence Grove Forest Preserve

BOSACKI'S HOME BREW

FIELD NOTES

610 E. Hawley St.
Mundelein, IL 60060
224-778-5400
**bosackishomebrew.
com**

Named after owner Greg Bosacki, he and his wife Brigitte decided to take his homebrewing hobby to the next level in 2015. While beer can be consumed on premise, the space and mission still lean towards taking beer home to enjoy. Focusing on traditional styles featuring wheat ales, they have both year round beers along with many seasonal options. In addition to their passion for beer, they have great dedication to their local community, hosting events and fundraisers for multiple organizations around Mundelein.

OWNER
Greg Bosacki,
Brigitte Bosacki

HEAD BREWER
Greg Bosacki

AVAILABILITY
Taproom only

BEST KNOWN FOR
Sessionable
American styles,
German wheat ales

DATE FOUNDED
2015

PUBLIC TRANSIT
NCS/Mundelein

| 12 | 69 | | | • | • | • | | • | • | 4.0/5 |

BOSACKI'S HOME BREW

PRO TIPS

» Wednesdays are $1 off pints.

» While snacks are limited to the free popcorn available, bringing your own food is always an option.

» Greg himself is usually tending bar; ask him to help you complete one of the many puzzles available.

» Occasionally, they invite guest brewers (home brewers) to share their recipes.

DATE OF VISIT:

MY RATING
☆ ☆ ☆ ☆ ☆

NOTES:

POPULAR BEERS

Back Porch Porter	I Wish Red Ale	Base- ment Bavarian Wheat	Word To The Weizen- bock

M	Tu	W	Th	F	S	Su
closed	closed	4-9p	4-9p	3-10p	2-10p	2-6p

BUFFALO CREEK BREWING

FIELD NOTES

360 Historical Ln.
Long Grove, IL 60047
847-821-6140
**buffalocreekbrewing.
com**

Buffalo Creek Brewing is part of the revitalization of downtown Long Grove, a village with New England-style charm and many independent small businesses. The brewery undertook a massive renovation of a former art gallery space on Historical Lane to create an inviting Bavarian style taproom with plenty of long wooden benches and a large outdoor beer garden. Quaint doesn't begin to describe it. The beers, though, mean business. As one might expect, the beer list leans less on esoteric picks to focus more on brews that can capture and captivate a wide audience.

OWNER	DATE FOUNDED
Mike Marr	2017

HEAD BREWER	KEY EVENTS
Mike Marr	St. Patrick's Day (Mar)

AVAILABILITY
Draft only - limited

BEST KNOWN FOR
German and Belgian styles

12 | 120 | • | • | • | • | • | | • | | 3.9/5

BUFFALO CREEK BREWING

PRO TIPS

» When inside, you'll feel as if you're in a homey log cabin with wood throughout. Among the various seating options, they have beer barrels that have been turned into four-top tables.

» Long Grove hosts numerous big festivals so Craft Beer Fest (Apr), Chocolate Fest (May), Strawberry Fest (Jun) and Apple Fest (Sept) are all excellent times to plan a visit.

» Live music every Saturday night. Other regular events include Sip & Paint workshops and trivia nights.

» Many breweries have event spaces but few can compare with the 2nd level private space that can hold groups up to 130 guests.

POPULAR BEERS

Marrvel-ous	360 Pils	Burning Red	42K

DATE OF VISIT:

MY RATING
☆ ☆ ☆ ☆ ☆

NOTES:

M	Tu	W	Th	F	S	Su
4-10p	4-10p	4-10p	4-10p	12-11p	11a-11p	12-6p

CRYSTAL LAKE BREWING

FIELD NOTES

150 N. Main St.
Crystal Lake, IL
60014
779-220-9288
crystallakebrew.com

The town of Crystal Lake abuts Crystal Lake itself, as well as the Three Oaks Recreational Area, so you can bet that rest and relaxation are things that Crystal Lake Brewing takes seriously. You can imagine drinking these beers while boating or lazing on an inner tube. The life-preserver imagery on their cans goes hand-in-hand with their mantra of "beer that is easy to drink, and hard to put down." Their brewing philosophy is serious, though, with German ingredients imported for their blonde lager and plenty of care given to their Boathouse series of rare and barrel-aged beers.

OWNER
Chuck Ross, John O'Fallon

HEAD BREWER
Ryan Clooney

AVAILABILITY
N. IL

BEST KNOWN FOR
Blonde lagers, IPAs, pale ales

DATE FOUNDED
2014

RECENT AWARDS
WBC 2016

KEY EVENTS
Maibock Festival (Spring), Oktoberfest (Fall)

PUBLIC TRANSIT
UP-NW/Crystal Lake

12 | 180 | • | • | • | • | • | | | • | | • | 3.8/5

CRYSTAL LAKE BREWING

PRO TIPS

» Dog friendly on the patio only.

» Flights come with a smart, stylish presentation: a circular wooden paddle shaped like a life preserver.

» There's often live music on Thursdays, and food trucks are known to come by on Fridays.

» A well-lit patio provides a unique, nighttime atmosphere that almost feels like it could be your neighbor's back yard.

» Tours are available Saturdays at 2p; the $10 price includes a beer and a take-home tumbler.

» Children permitted until 7p.

DATE OF VISIT:

MY RATING
☆ ☆ ☆ ☆ ☆

NOTES:

POPULAR BEERS

M	Tu	W	Th	F	S	Su
4-10p	4-10p	4-10p	4-10p	3p-12a	12p-12a	12-9p

EMMETT'S BREWING CO.

FIELD NOTES

128 W. Main St.
West Dundee, IL
60118
847-428-4500
**emmettsbrewingco.
com**

Founder Andy Burns got his first taste of craft beer while attending Marquette University in Milwaukee. The boss at his summer job would hand him one of his home brews at the end of the shift for the two of them to share, and soon Burns was making trips to the local homebrew store himself. After a stint on the west coast in the Marines, witnessing the boom of craft beer in that hop-heavy part of the world, Burns' wish became to help pioneer a craft beer boom of his own in his native Chicagoland, naming the venture after his grandfather, Emmett in 1999.

Emmett's Brewing

OWNER	**DATE FOUNDED**
Andrew Burns	1999
HEAD BREWER	**RECENT AWARDS**
Dennis Abplanalp	GABF 2016, 2017
AVAILABILITY	**KEY EVENTS**
Chicago	Quarterly
BEST KNOWN FOR	Beermaster dinners,
IPAs, German ales	St. Patrick's Day
and lagers	(Mar), New Year's
	Eve (Dec)

12 | 170 | • | • | • | • | • | | • | • | | 3.6/5

EMMETT'S BREWING CO.

PRO TIPS

» Visit their other locations at: 110 N. Brockway St., Palatine, IL; 121 W. Front St., Wheaton, IL; 5200 Main St., Downers Grove, IL.

» Dog friendly on the patio only.

» Each of the four locations have friendly, main street-style architecture that integrates well into Emmett's small-town, neighborhood pub ethos.

» Expect a large, family-friendly food menu that offers plenty of crowd-pleasing appetizers and small bites in various permutations, salads, sandwiches, burgers, and entrées.

» An in-house mug club will get one a special glass to drink from in-house, plus other periodic benefits.

Emmett's Brewing

DATE OF VISIT:

MY RATING
☆ ☆ ☆ ☆ ☆

NOTES:

POPULAR BEERS

M	Tu	W	Th	F	S	Su
11:30-11	11:30-11	11:30-11	11:30-11	11:30-12	11:30-12	11:30-9

FLESK BREWING

FIELD NOTES

James and William O'Brien, owners of Flesk Brewing, both attended the Siebel Institute together after they decided to put sibling rivalries aside and go into the brewing business together. They used to operate a production facility in Lombard in the Western suburbs but in 2016, they completed a relocation to Barrington in the Northwest suburbs. The focus of the new space is a nice-sized taproom that opened in 2017 in the Ice House Mall, just a short walk from the Barrington Metra stop. Expect a variety of IPAs plus plenty of sessionable styles as well. But unfortunately, no sword fight nights.

200 Applebee St., Ste E
Barrington, IL 60010
224-665-7291
fleskbrewing.com

OWNER
William O'Brien,
James O'Brien

HEAD BREWER
James O'Brien

AVAILABILITY
Taproom only

BEST KNOWN FOR
IPAs, milk stouts,
helles lagers

DATE FOUNDED
2013

PUBLIC TRANSIT
UP-NW/Barrington

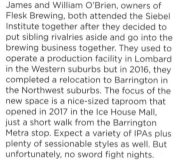

10 | 161 | • | • | • | • | • | | • | | • | 4.0/5

FLESK BREWING

PRO TIPS

» The Ice House Mall got its name from Bowman Dairy, the company that formerly inhabited the 1904 facility. The red brick of the now-mall space gives all the housed businesses a genuine feel that one simply does not get from most suburban shopping facilities.

» The semi-circular entrance to Flesk from the outside of Ice House Mall is the sort of vaulted entryway that most other brewery spaces would dream of. The inside is well-lit and friendly despite the relative lack of windows.

» Musicians and food vendors have been known to come in fairly regularly. There are also themed trivia nights.

DATE OF VISIT:

MY RATING
☆ ☆ ☆ ☆ ☆

NOTES:

POPULAR BEERS

Coat Of Arms	Running Man Milk Stout	Big Pointy Teeth	Front Toward Enemy

M	Tu	W	Th	F	S	Su
closed	3-10p	3-10p	3-10p	3p-12a	12p-12a	12-10p

LIGHT THE LAMP BREWERY

FIELD NOTES

2 S. Lake St.
Grayslake, IL 60030
847-752-8489
**lightthelampbrewery.
com**

The people behind every brewery come together for a wide variety of reasons. This uniqueness holds true for the hockey dads of Grayslake. They always wanted a place to huddle warmly together and watch hockey, all while drinking some amazing beer. The reality of this brainchild saw its fruition in 2012 with Light The Lamp Brewery. Dan Ray, their head brewer, puts together a wide variety of styles that appeal to hockey fans and all others. And they must be on to something as they expand into a much larger space for 2018.

OWNER
Bill Hermes, Jeff
Sheppard, Dave
Cavanaugh

HEAD BREWER
Dan Ray

AVAILABILITY
Taproom only

BEST KNOWN FOR
Sours, variety

DATE FOUNDED
2012

2017 PRODUCTION
251 bbl

KEY EVENTS
Pond Hockey
Tournament (Jan),
Chili Cookoff (Nov)

20 | 150 | | • | • | • | | • | • | | 3.8/5

LIGHT THE LAMP BREWERY

PRO TIPS

» 2018 is a big year for Light the Lamp with an expansion of space, addition of a full food menu (including Saturday/Sunday brunch), and the addition of wine, spirits, ciders and a beer engine.

» They still like hockey here (a lot), but their true passion is letting great beer take center stage.

» Like trivia? Head over on Tuesdays. Like bingo, head over on Wednesdays.

» Great meetup space after checking out the fantastic Grayslake farmers market during summer weekends.

» Stay tuned for their launch into the distribution game later in 2018 for both draft and cans.

DATE OF VISIT:

MY RATING
☆ ☆ ☆ ☆ ☆

NOTES:

POPULAR BEERS

Short-handed Hazy IPA	Dr. Funke	Still Single

M	Tu	W	Th	F	S	Su
11a-12a	11a-12a	11a-12a	11a-12a	11a-12a	9a-12a	9a-12a

THE LUCKY MONK

FIELD NOTES

South Barrington may be a ways from the city proper, but that doesn't mean its denizens don't deserve a brewpub that combines the comfort food of a local bar with house-made brews and large patio area with requisite fire pit. Lucky Monk generally offers five perennial beers and one seasonal offering for customers, in addition to six or so guest taps. Named after Belgian Trappist monks, these guys take both their beer and food very seriously, some may say to the religious experience level.

105 Hollywood Blvd.
South Barrington, IL
60010
847-898-0500
theluckymonk.com

OWNER
Samatas family

HEAD BREWER
Anthony Carolio

AVAILABILITY
Brewpub only

BEST KNOWN FOR
German styles, IPAs, stouts

DATE FOUNDED
2009

| 12 | 400 | • | | | • | • | | • | • | | 3.7/5 |

THE LUCKY MONK

PRO TIPS

» Check out the Monk Society, a frequent-customer program that lets customers earn points with each purchase, and redeem points for rewards. The Society also offers discounts on growlers, bombers, and kegs to-go, plus a complimentary birthday burger, a mug, and priority seating.

» Suburban comfort and friendliness exude from the exterior before you even enter from the huge parking lot. Edison bulbs and wooden ceiling beams allow for a bit of style to triumph over suburban homogeneity.

» Try the sticky donuts for dessert.

» They have happy hour Mon-Thurs 3-6p featuring $3.50 pints and food specials.

POPULAR BEERS

Confessional IPA	Fallen Angel	Trittica Wheat Ale	Solitude Oatmeal Stout

M	Tu	W	Th	F	S	Su
11a-11p	11a-11p	11a-11p	11a-11p	11a-1a	11a-1a	11a-11p

DATE OF VISIT:

MY RATING
☆ ☆ ☆ ☆ ☆

NOTES:

MIKERPHONE BREWING

FIELD NOTES

121 Garlisch Dr.
Elk Grove Village, IL
60007
847-264-8904
**mikerphonebrewing.
com**

Mikerphone, currently one of the Chicagoland area's buzziest breweries, is helmed by Mike Pallen. Pallen is a music industry veteran, doing everything from promoting and managing bands, to helping run the international marketing for School of Rock. Mike was previously the head brewer at the now defunct BreakRoom Brewery and SlapShot Brewing Company, along with stints at Pipeworks and 18th Street. His current venture has led him to produce several highly lauded and in-demand beers that generate plenty of excitement with each release.

OWNER
Mike Pallen, Lisa
Pallen

HEAD BREWER
Mike Pallen

AVAILABILITY
Chicago - very
limited

BEST KNOWN FOR
NE IPAs, sours,
stouts

DATE FOUNDED
2015

KEY EVENTS
Smells Like a Beer
Fest (Spring)

8 | 45 | | | • | • | | | | 4.2/5

MIKERPHONE BREWING

PRO TIPS

» Bottles currently see extremely limited distribution, so if you want this nectar, make sure you're willing to brave a line at the taproom (especially on the weekends) or find a store off the beaten path.

» Located in a friendly industrial park, the taproom itself is around 1,000 square feet and features plenty of guitars and amps lining the walls. The space is bright and kid-friendly.

» Bottle releases generally lead to the biggest crowds at Mikerphone, so prepare yourself if you're going during a release.

» The bottles-to-go line forms at the left door, while the taproom line forms at the right door (where you can purchase bottles-to-go as well)

POPULAR BEERS

DATE OF VISIT:

MY RATING
☆☆☆☆☆

NOTES:

M	Tu	W	Th	F	S	Su
3-8p	closed	3-8p	3-10p	12-10p	11a-10p	11a-7p

ROARING TABLE BREWING CO.

FIELD NOTES

739 W. Route 22
Lake Zurich, IL 60047
224-662-4562
roaringtable.com

Lane Fearing took up homebrewing after being laid off from an advertising gig. When his wife asked him "Why not just be a beer guy," he took it to heart. Fearing went to the Siebel Institute and then brewed for nine years at Mickey Finn's in Libertyville. Roaring Table features an eclectic variety of small-batch, delicately-crafted brews that showcase many flavors. And the taproom is an elegant, stylish space that could easily be mistaken as a trendy nightspot in a posh, downtown Chicago neighborhood.

Jack Muldowney

OWNER
Lane Fearing, Beth
May

DATE FOUNDED
2017

HEAD BREWER
Lane Fearing

AVAILABILITY
Taproom only

BEST KNOWN FOR
NE IPAs, Foeder
sours, stouts

12 | 122 | • | • | • | • | • | | • | | 4.2/5

ROARING TABLE BREWING CO.

PRO TIPS

» Dog friendly on the patio only.

» This is a taproom where you can wear a sport jacket or a fancy dress to and not feel out of place. The round mirrors behind the bar, fireplace lounge, stylish lighting fixtures, and live-edge ash bar almost obscure the fact that it's essentially in the middle of a shopping mall.

» Roaring Tables also features a selection of small batch cider, boutique wines and Kombucha.

» Expect food trucks and live music on the weekends.

Jack Muldowney

DATE OF VISIT:

MY RATING
☆ ☆ ☆ ☆ ☆

NOTES:

POPULAR BEERS

Tuba Solo	Canadian Girl-friend	Sugar-beam

M	Tu	W	Th	F	S	Su
closed	closed	3-10p	3-10p	3p-12a	12p-12a	12-8p

SCORCHED EARTH BREWING COMPANY

FIELD NOTES

Mike Dallas, with the loving kindness, and support of his wife (and brewery co-owner) Jen, started up Scorched Earth in their home in McHenry County after Mike completed past employment lives in the Air Force and public administration. Scorched Earth sports a 15-barrel system in the northwestern suburb of Algonquin. The beers themselves run the gamut from American to Belgian, hoppy to mild, dark to light, and everywhere in between.

203 Berg St.
Algonquin, IL 60102
224-209-8472
scorchedearthbrew-ing.com

OWNER
Mike Dallas, Jennifer Dallas

HEAD BREWER
Mark Gres

AVAILABILITY
Chicago, IA

BEST KNOWN FOR
Sours, barrel aged beers, variety using local fruit

DATE FOUNDED
2014

RECENT AWARDS
FoBAB 2016

KEY EVENTS
Scorched Earth Day (Jun)

| 12 | 50 | • | • | • | • | | | | • | | 4.0/5 |

SCORCHED EARTH BREWING COMPANY

PRO TIPS

» Dog friendly on the patio only.

» The sizable space has a long bar with plenty of seating, as well as picnic or beer hall-style tables that offer a view of the brewery setup. New semi-private event space.

» While there's no kitchen, there are plenty of good restaurants close-by for ordering food in.

» Get in line for the shuffleboard table if you feel like you can hustle your friends.

» Trivia nights are on Thursdays at the taproom, with food trucks occasionally coming by on Fridays.

» Live music periodically at the tap room, but check ahead to see if there's a show.

POPULAR BEERS

DATE OF VISIT:

MY RATING
☆ ☆ ☆ ☆ ☆

NOTES:

M	Tu	W	Th	F	S	Su
closed	closed	3-10p	3-10p	3-10p	12-10p	12-7p

SIDE LOT BREWERY

FIELD NOTES

Up in Wauconda, IL, Side Lot provides its guests with a small stable of four perennial brews, a good selection of seasonal options, and a special release every now and then to make the geeks happy. Next to a gas station in a literal side lot, the space offers some well-curated guest drafts and European-inspired sandwiches. A variety of small plates complement their house brews nicely. And if you're not feeling like a beer, grab one of the ciders available instead.

110 Slocum Lake Rd.
Wauconda, IL
60084
847-865-0281
sidelotbrewing.com

OWNER
Phil Castello,
Brittany Barth,
Jason Vucic

HEAD BREWER
Phil Castello

AVAILABILITY
Brewpub only

BEST KNOWN FOR
IPAs, range of
European styles

DATE FOUNDED
2015

16 | 60 | • | • | | • | | | • | • | | 3.5/5

SIDE LOT BREWERY

PRO TIPS

» Dog friendly on the patio only (which is huge at 85 seats).

» The entrance is off the side lot near the Citgo station in Wauconda, but the space itself is leisurely and inviting, with couches, TVs, and bar seating aplenty.

» Beer and yoga is hosted every month or so, and the cost covers some beer after the class is done.

» The food menu is carefully put together with some surprisingly fancy offerings. Candied bacon and a bacon jam small plate both make the carnivore's mouth water, while whipped feta with pepper jelly and fresh bread is downright decadent.

DATE OF VISIT:

MY RATING
☆ ☆ ☆ ☆ ☆

NOTES:

POPULAR BEERS

Jimmy The Weasel

Cocky Woodpecker IPA

Smokin' Squirrel

M	Tu	W	Th	F	S	Su
closed	3-11p	3-11p	3-11p	3p-12a	11a-1a	11a-8p

TIGHTHEAD BREWING COMPANY

FIELD NOTES

Tighthead's tagline is "worth more than a try" and for this north-suburban brewery, they've proven themselves more than up to the task. Owner and head brewer Bruce Dir got the itch for brewing in 1993, when his then-fiancée/now-wife gave him a homebrew kit for Christmas. Eighteen years and an education at the Siebel Institute of Technology later, Tighthead Brewing opened in Mundelein in 2011. The name "Tighthead" is a rugby position term, thus explaining the flaming rugby ball in the brewery's logo.

161 N. Archer Ave.
Mundelein, IL 60060
847-970-9174
tightheadbrewing.com

OWNER
Bruce Dir

HEAD BREWER
Billy Oaks

AVAILABILITY
IL, WI

BEST KNOWN FOR
IPAs, pales, reds, Belgians

DATE FOUNDED
2011

2017 PRODUCTION
3,000 bbl

KEY EVENTS
Mundelein Beer Fest (Jun), Hoptoberfest (Sept)

PUBLIC TRANSIT
NCS/Mundelein

16 | 140 | • | • | • | • | • | | • | 4.0/5

TIGHTHEAD BREWING COMPANY

PRO TIPS

» "Pints and Poses" is Tighthead's monthly yoga series on each first Sunday. $20 will get you an hour of yoga and 2 pints at the taproom.

» The brewery's merchandise store features prints of can label art, hand-crafted beer soap, label-themed Swiss Army knives, and even logo-emblazoned rugby balls for the aspiring rugger in the family.

» Major supporter of the Mundelein Craft Beer Festival, which celebrated its 6th iteration in June 2017.

» Board games are available. On Wednesdays they have trivia and live music Thursdays and occasionally on the weekends.

DATE OF VISIT:

MY RATING
☆ ☆ ☆ ☆ ☆

NOTES:

POPULAR BEERS

M	Tu	W	Th	F	S	Su
4-10p	4-10p	4-10p	4-10p	12-11p	12-11p	12-6p

VILLAGE VINTNER WINERY & BREWERY

FIELD NOTES

2380 Esplanade Dr.
Algonquin, IL 60102
847-658-4900
**thevillagevintner.
com**

Doesn't a vintner make wine? Yes. So, what is Village Vintner, a winery that's been around since 2005 doing in a taproom guide? Well, they decided just crafting wine wasn't enough and opened up a brewery in 2012, making them the only such combination business in the entire area. Housed in a huge space in Algonquin, this combination facility also sports a wood-fired oven for pizzas and other entrées.

OWNER
Steve Boyer, Bob Boyer

HEAD BREWER
Steve Boyer, Brett Boyer

AVAILABILITY
Brewpub only

BEST KNOWN FOR
IPAs, cream ales, British styles

DATE FOUNDED
2012

12 | 125 | • | | • | • | | • | • | | 3.6/5

VILLAGE VINTNER WINERY & BREWERY

PRO TIPS

» The space is a multi-level suburban brick building that features plenty of bar seating and tables.

» The food menu makes use of the wood-fired oven, sure, but check out the mozzarella-prosciutto roll; they're made daily.

» A more adventurous person might suggest opting for the cashew and pear pizza or pesto and asparagus instead of a standard red pie, or you have the choice of designing your own pizza, too.

» The wine and growler club is free to join, and offers a discount on the monthly purchase of bottles or a growler, plus a tasting of beers or wines.

DATE OF VISIT:

MY RATING
☆ ☆ ☆ ☆ ☆

NOTES:

POPULAR BEERS

| Hoprock-et IPA | Coconilla Stout | Vanilla Cream Ale | Bourbon Barrel Aged Ale |

M	Tu	W	Th	F	S	Su
5-10p	11a-10p	11a-10p	11a-10p	11-11:30	11-11:30	12-9p

WILD ONION BREWERY

FIELD NOTES

22221 N. Pepper Rd.
Lake Barrington, IL
60010
847-381-7308
onionbrewery.com

Wild Onion Brewery began in 1996 as a production-only operation, but the idea of opening a brewpub always lingered in minds of the Kainz family. The original 1996 brewery was constructed out of old dairy equipment in a warehouse. Today, the production brewery sits below the pub itself among a 20-acre complex (a former gravel quarry) that houses the Onion Brewery's green initiative. The restoration turned what had been an impromptu dump into a beautiful nature site.

OWNER
Mike Kainz, John Kainz

HEAD BREWER
Peter Janusas

AVAILABILITY
IL, KS, NJ, NY, PA

BEST KNOWN FOR
IPAs, stouts

DATE FOUNDED
1996

RECENT AWARDS
FoBAB 2016

| 18 | 135 | • | | | • | • | • | | • | • | | 3.6/5 |

WILD ONION BREWERY

PRO TIPS

» Visit their other location at: 1111 South Blvd., Oak Park, IL (new).

» The woodwork inside this lodge-like complex of brewpub and banquet hall is simply stunning. Featuring some rescued timbers from the Revolutionary War era, the Onion pub features a large, intricately cut, multi-sided bar that has plenty of seating and even a stone fireplace in the middle of the pub.

» The menu has just enough variations on the pub grub theme to keep it interesting.

» The pub's Great Hall is a huge reception space used mainly for weddings. When it's booked (most weekends in the summer), the outdoor space is closed. So call ahead.

POPULAR BEERS

DATE OF VISIT:

MY RATING
☆ ☆ ☆ ☆ ☆

NOTES:

M	Tu	W	Th	F	S	Su
closed	11a-11p	11a-11p	11a-11p	11a-12a	11a-12a	11a-8p

SUBURBS WEST

1. 5 Rabbit
2. Alter
3. Black Horizon
4. Blue Nose
5. BuckleDown
6. Church Street
7. Elmhurst
8. Exit Strategy
9. Flapjack
10. Imperial Oak
11. Itasca
12. Kinslahger
13. Lunar
14. Miskatonic
15. More
16. Myths and Legends
17. Noon Whistle Brewing
18. Oak Park Brewing Co.
19. Short Fuse Brewing
20. Skeleton Key Brewery

NEIGHBORHOOD HIGHLIGHTS

1 O'Hare Int'l Airport
2 Midway Int'l Airport
3 Toyota Park
4 Frank Lloyd Wright Home & Studio
5 Brookfield Zoo

I-290

Cicero

I-55

5 RABBIT CERVECERIA

FIELD NOTES

6398 W. 74th St.
Bedford Park, IL
60638
312-895-9591
5rabbitbrewery.com

5 Rabbit is the United States' first Latin American-inspired brewery. The brewery's creative director, Randy Mosher, is one of Chicago's legends of craft beer and author of one of the definitive craft beer tomes, Tasting Beer. 5 Rabbit's beers take inspiration from Latin American culture and cuisine for their unique flavors and style choices. In June 2016, 5 Rabbit gained national press for their blonde ale, Chinga tu Pelo, a not-at-all subtle jibe at a certain presidential candidate's infamous coiffure.

OWNER
Andres Araya,
Randy Mosher

HEAD BREWER
Nathan Chesser

AVAILABILITY
Chicago, FL, IN, OH

BEST KNOWN FOR
Fruit beers, lighter
styles

DATE FOUNDED
2011

RECENT AWARDS
FoBAB 2016

8 | 80 | • | • | • | | | | • | | 3.8/5

5 RABBIT CERVECERIA

PRO TIPS

» Cleverly nicknamed "The Rabbit Hole," 5 Rabbit's Bedford Park facility is less than two miles from Toyota Park, home of MLS' Chicago Fire, so combining both experiences into one day would make for an ideal suburban excursion.

» Latin American inspired artwork adorns the space, which features several tables, but no bar seating.

» Movies on the wall and a foosball table are available for entertainment.

» Look for beers with culinary flair, featuring spices and foods from Latin America.

» Food trucks will occasionally show up, but the taproom is BYOF, too.

» Each week they release a taproom only beer.

DATE OF VISIT:

MY RATING
☆ ☆ ☆ ☆ ☆

NOTES:

POPULAR BEERS

M	Tu	W	Th	F	S	Su
closed	closed	4-10p	4-10p	4-11p	1-9p	closed

ALTER BREWING COMPANY

FIELD NOTES

2300 Wisconsin
Ave., Ste. 213
Downers Grove, IL
60515
630-541-9558
alterbrewing.com

Alter opened in 2015, bringing craft beer to the western suburb of Downers Grove. The taproom features 12 drafts that run the gamut of styles, taste profiles, and alcohol strengths with an impressive level of economy. Hopheads and dark beer fans will be pleased alongside sour aficionados and drinkers of session beers. The space itself features a high ceiling, plenty of seating at the bar, a "roomy-industrial space" that gets accents from orange chairs and plenty of wood accents, especially behind the bar. For a suburban taproom, this looks and feels pretty hip.

OWNER
Mark Hedrick,
David Yob,
Pete Kosanovich

HEAD BREWER
Mark Hedrick

AVAILABILITY
Chicago

BEST KNOWN FOR
IPAs, BA varieties

DATE FOUNDED
2015

2017 PRODUCTION
1,660 bbl

RECENT AWARDS
FoBAB 2016, 2017

KEY EVENTS
Alter Fest (Fall),
Anniversary Party
(Dec)

PUBLIC TRANSIT
BNSF/Belmont

| 12 | 106 | | | • | | • | | • | | | • | | • | | 3.9/5 |

ALTER BREWING COMPANY

PRO TIPS

» Alter features trivia every Tuesday night. Yoga sessions also take place periodically on Saturdays, with an hour of yoga and a beer offered for a combined $15.

» No food menu, but food trucks do come occasionally.

» It should be noted that, like some other suburban breweries, Alter has a 48 ounce per person limit on beer that can be served on site, so, as their menu says, choose wisely.

» If you're looking to join the growler club it only opens up once a year, so you'd better get on it fast. The club offers different perks each year.

» Check out their Barrel Room and Loft for your private events.

DATE OF VISIT:

MY RATING
☆ ☆ ☆ ☆ ☆

NOTES:

POPULAR BEERS

King Balaton

M	Tu	W	Th	F	S	Su
3-10p	3-10p	3-10p	3-10p	12-11p	12-11p	12-7p

BLACK HORIZON BREWING COMPANY

FIELD NOTES

The name Black Horizon might conjure images of mythical creatures or galactic phenomenons, but it's meaning is actually more simple and direct. "Every business wants to be in the black eventually and that's on our horizon. Get it?" Works for us. Willowbrook's first brewery currently offers a modest yet exciting selection of beers that chart their own path.

7560 S. Quincy St.
Willowbrook, IL 60527
630-413-4964
blackhorizonbrewing. com

OWNER
Kevin Baldus,
Charles St. Clair,
Alex Stankus

HEAD BREWER
Alex Stankus

AVAILABILITY
Limited - draft only

BEST KNOWN FOR
IPAs, pale ales,
stouts

DATE FOUNDED
2016

8 | 65 | • | • | • | • | • | | | • | | 3.9/5

BLACK HORIZON BREWING COMPANY

PRO TIPS

» Dog friendly on the patio only.

» Black Horizon is in a industrial park so follow your GPS and look for the A frame sign to turn into the parking lot.

» Board games, video games (including an old-school Nintendo 64) and a foosball table are available.

» Batches are small enough at Black Horizon that one shouldn't expect a favorite beer to last too long before something else takes its place, though the plan is to eventually increase production on fan favorites.

» Trivia nights on 2nd and 4th Thursdays of the month.

» Credit card only, no cash.

POPULAR BEERS

| Fool Me Once | Campfire Fun | Straight Up | Blood Moon Prophecy |

DATE OF VISIT:

MY RATING

NOTES:

M	Tu	W	Th	F	S	Su
closed	closed	3-10p	3-11p	12-11p	12-11p	12-7p

25

BLUE NOSE BREWERY

FIELD NOTES

6119 East Ave.
Hodgkins, IL 60525
708-905-5198
bluenosebrewery.com

A suburban strip mall in Hodgkins, IL, is the setting for Blue Nose, formerly of the equally small town of Justice, both in the southwest suburbs. Blue Nose has been known to collaborate with other breweries, including Tim Hoerman's 51st Ward Brewing. The two collaborated on a Cubs-themed barrel-aged saison simply called "The 2016." It was brewed on Opening Day and bottled during the now-famous, losing streak-ending World Series. Blue Nose is meant to be a neighborhood gathering place that strives to be "spacious yet cozy," fitting for its suburban audience.

OWNER
Nathan Garcia,
Jordan Isenberg

HEAD BREWER
Jordan Isenberg,
Justin Rigoni

AVAILABILITY
Chicago - limited

BEST KNOWN FOR
Belgians, pales, IPAs

DATE FOUNDED
2012

| 10 | 250 | • | • | • | • | | | • | | 4.0/5 |

BLUE NOSE BREWERY

PRO TIPS

» The taproom is a bright, friendly space with brushed-metal furniture and a bright blue floor in the brewing space.

» Chicago sports teams get plenty of screen time with sound on the big screen.

» Periodically hosts tournaments of favorite old school video games.

» The brewery's dog, also featured in the logo of the brewery, is a semi-regular visitor to the space.

» Blue Nose often partners with the Ofrenda food truck, offering a semi-traditional Taco Tuesday that's always a crowd pleaser.

» They have a pool table and cornhole set to entertain while drinking.

DATE OF VISIT:

MY RATING
☆ ☆ ☆ ☆ ☆

NOTES:

POPULAR BEERS

Archer Ave.	Saison Sarandon	XXX Honey	The Other

M	Tu	W	Th	F	S	Su
3p-12a	3p-12a	3p-12a	3p-12a	12p-2a	12p-2a	12-10p

BUCKLEDOWN BREWING

FIELD NOTES

8700 W. 47th St.
Lyons, IL 60534
708-777-1842
**buckledownbrewing.
com**

Sean Mahoney and Ike Orcutt founded BuckleDown in the small southwestern suburb of Lyons, with an ethos similar to that of their surroundings: hard working, honest people looking to make the sorts of beers that they like to drink themselves. Their beers are a studied mix of hop-forward American styles and observantly made Belgian ales. Their main flagship beers are drinkable, proletarian, and hop-forward. Beyond the flagships, don't miss their collaboration beers with places like Kuma's, Greenbush and Haymarket.

OWNER
Sean Mahoney, Ike Orcutt

HEAD BREWER
Ike Orcutt

AVAILABILITY
Chicago, NW IN

BEST KNOWN FOR
Pales, IPAs, seasonal lagers

DATE FOUNDED
2013

2017 PRODUCTION
2,500 bbl

KEY EVENTS
Oktoberfest (Sept), Grapefruit Belt and Suspenders Release (Jun)

| 10 | 75 | | | • | | • | | | | | | • | | 3.9/5 |

BUCKLEDOWN BREWING

PRO TIPS

» Bright yellow stools at the bar are the first thing that catches the eye at the otherwise wood, metal, and concrete-adorned taproom.

» Plenty of taproom exclusives can be had in addition to the normal roll call of flagship and perennial beers.

» Live music is a feature almost every weekend.

» There may not be outdoor seating, but the big garage door to the brewery opens to let some breeze and sunshine in.

» Their big annual release is for Barrel-Aged Shadowbox; typically a few variants of Shadowbox are on draft only at the tap room.

» Food trucks on the weekends.

POPULAR BEERS

DATE OF VISIT:

MY RATING
☆ ☆ ☆ ☆ ☆

NOTES:

M	Tu	W	Th	F	S	Su
4-10p	4-10p	4-10p	12-11p	12-11p	12-11p	12-5p

CHURCH STREET BREWING COMPANY

FIELD NOTES

1480 Industrial Dr.
Itasca, IL 60143
630-438-5725
churchstreetbrew.com

Located 10 miles west of Chicago in suburban Itasca, Church Street specializes mostly in continental European styles that don't often see production in the United States, let alone in Chicago. Sure, the Brimstone IPA is the bone they throw to those who firmly believe that an American brewery simply cannot exist without a hoppy offering, but dig deeper and you'll find some lovely examples of styles that you'd normally only find fresh across the pond.

OWNER
Lisa Gregor, Joe Gregor

HEAD BREWER
TJ Bachorz

AVAILABILITY
IL, FL, MO

BEST KNOWN FOR
Lagers, pilsners, seasonal German styles

DATE FOUNDED
2012

2017 PRODUCTION
2,300 bbl

8 | 150 | • | • | • | | | | • | | 3.9/5

CHURCH STREET BREWING COMPANY

PRO TIPS

» Cinder block walls get adorned with plenty of decorative bottles, metal tack signs, and hung frames, turning what could be a drab industrial space into an inviting, busy, and friendly taproom that proclaims "NO WORKING DURING DRINKING HOURS."

» Seating is a couple of modest folding tables, picnic tables, and some barrels with stools surrounding; it's minimal but homey.

» Food trucks will come by occasionally, but otherwise there's no kitchen.

» Ping-pong table available and live music most Saturdays for entertainment.

DATE OF VISIT:

MY RATING
☆ ☆ ☆ ☆ ☆

NOTES:

POPULAR BEERS

M	Tu	W	Th	F	S	Su
5-10p	5-10p	5-10p	5-10p	4-11p	12-11p	12-7p

ELMHURST BREWING COMPANY

FIELD NOTES

171 N. Addison Ave.
Elmhurst, IL 60126
630-834-2739
**elmhurstbrewing-
company.com**

A short walk from the Elmhurst train station, Elmhurst Brewing offers a full brewpub menu and 13 drafts. Pete Dolan and Frazer Donaldson are the minds behind Elmhurst Brewing, who believe that the Western suburb has an ardent craft beer fanbase thirsty for a place to call their own. They opened in 2017 with a unique mix of lagers and ales that are thoughtfully constructed from low-complexity to high, and that pair well with their menu of upscale pub food.

OWNER
Frazer Donaldson,
Pete Dolan

HEAD BREWER
Cam Horn

AVAILABILITY
Brewpub only

BEST KNOWN FOR
German style lagers
and ales, coffee
stout

DATE FOUNDED
2017

KEY EVENTS
Oktoberfest (Sept)

PUBLIC TRANSIT
UP-W/Elmhurst

13 | 150 | • | • | | • | • | • | | • | • | • | 3.8/5

ELMHURST BREWING COMPANY

PRO TIPS

» A modestly-stylish interior lets you know you're in a forward-thinking yet welcoming place.

» The food menu is well-executed and includes a variety of sauces and batters that incorporate Elmhurst's brews.

» Cask beers get tapped on Thursdays.

» A large outdoor beer garden features live music during the summer.

» Pair with a visit to the Elmhurst Art Museum which hosts a variety of cool exhibits throughout the year.

» Only Mug Club members are able to try the fabled "13th Tap."

» Drinks menu also features cocktails, spirits, wine and cider.

DATE OF VISIT:

MY RATING
☆ ☆ ☆ ☆ ☆

NOTES:

POPULAR BEERS

Fools Gold	Go To Helles	Julius Squeezer	The Schwartz

M	Tu	W	Th	F	S	Su
closed	4-11p	4-11p	4-11p	4p-12a	11a-12a	11a-10p

EXIT STRATEGY BREWING CO.

FIELD NOTES

7700 Madison St.
Forest Park, IL
60130
708-689-8771
**exitstrategybrew-
ing.com**

Don't let the plain, rustic outside deter you from checking out this brewery. A short 10 minute walk from the Forest Park blue line stop, the inside will completely blow you away. As the first and only brewery in Forest Park, owner/brewmaster Chris Valleau and co-owner Katherine Valleau looked to create a nice blend of metropolitan living and suburban lifestyle. As a home brewer for many years winning over 40 awards across the country, their beers represent classic styles, modernized.

OWNER
Chris Valleau,
Katherine Valleau

HEAD BREWER
Chris Valleau

AVAILABILITY
Chicago - limited
draft only

BEST KNOWN FOR
IPAs, pales, fruit
beers, brown/
Scottish ales

DATE FOUNDED
2015

KEY EVENTS
Anniversary Party
(Apr)

PUBLIC TRANSIT
'L' Blue/Forest Park

16 | 140 | • | | • | | | • | • | • | 3.9/5

EXIT STRATEGY BREWING CO.

PRO TIPS

» Not feeling beer? They also have an entire list comprised of wine, cocktails and non-alcoholic options, including their own house made sodas.

» They offer an arrangement of food items from small plates and sandwiches to full blown meals (the burger is the best).

» Make sure to check out the overhead lamps at the bar. The bulb shades are different brewery growlers (Pintrest would approve).

» They have their mainstay beers but also have "lab beers" which are seasonal/one-offs.

» 21 and up only at the bar seats, but highchairs are available for future craft fans everywhere else.

DATE OF VISIT:

MY RATING
☆ ☆ ☆ ☆ ☆

NOTES:

POPULAR BEERS

| Judg-mental Dick | Perse-phone | Exit Strategy Pale Ale | Valleau-dated |

M	Tu	W	Th	F	S	Su
closed	3-10p	3-10p	3-10p	3p-12a	11a-12a	11a-4p

FLAPJACK BREWERY

FIELD NOTES

The "Established 2013" in the Flapjack logo is a reminder of how challenging it can be to open a brewery. It may have taken longer than expected for brothers Paul and James Macchione after they launched a Kickstarter campaign in 2014, but they finally opened their brewpub in May 2017 in Berwyn's Historic Depot District. The small batch brewery space features an open kitchen with a wood fired oven for a selection of neapolitan pizzas (prepared by James) to pair with your beers.

6833 Stanley Ave.
Berwyn, IL 60402
708-637-4030
**flapjackbrewery.
com**

OWNER
Paul Macchione,
James Macchione

HEAD BREWER
Paul Macchione

AVAILABILITY
Brewpub only

BEST KNOWN FOR
Lighter ales

DATE FOUNDED
2013

2017 PRODUCTION
107 bbl

PUBLIC TRANSIT
BNSF/Berwyn

8 | 60 | | | • | | | | • | | • | 3.9/5

FLAPJACK BREWERY

PRO TIPS

» This is a welcoming and friendly taproom with a simple character that keeps the focus on the beer.

» Flapjack was the owner Paul's nickname in high school due to his love of pancakes.

» Short walk from the Metra Berwyn stop. If driving, can pair with visits to Kinslahger, Oak Park Brewing and Exit Strategy.

» The family connection continues at Flapjack as brother-in-law Joey is the assistant brewer and a bartender.

DATE OF VISIT:

MY RATING
☆ ☆ ☆ ☆ ☆

NOTES:

POPULAR BEERS

| Fantasmo Vanilla Cream | Boltneck Coffee Stout | Dreamcrusher | Brumstache |

M	Tu	W	Th	F	S	Su
closed	closed	2-10p	2-10p	2-10p	12-10p	closed

IMPERIAL OAK BREWING

FIELD NOTES

501 Willow Blvd.
Willow Springs, IL
60480
708-330-5096
**imperialoakbrewing.
com**

Right off the Des Plaines (pronounced DEZZ PLAYNZ by the true Chicagoan) River, and minimal distance from several woods and nature preserves, Imperial Oak opened in 2014 with a small, 7-barrel system that allows for the production and release of plenty of new beers on a near-constant basis. The constant churn-and-burn of new beers coming on and off means that even regulars are treated to new options to taste with each visit. Options will range from the lighter, more universal crowd-pleasers to the heavy hitters for the initiated and voracious.

Grant Hamilton

OWNER
Grant Hamilton,
Chris DiBraccio,
Brett Semenske

HEAD BREWER
Brett Semenske

AVAILABILITY
Taproom only

BEST KNOWN FOR
IPAs, stouts, barrel
aged beers

DATE FOUNDED
2014

KEY EVENTS
Anniversary
Party (Jun), St.
Patrick's Day (Mar),
Oktoberfest (Sept)

PUBLIC TRANSIT
HC/Willow Springs

20 | 175 | • | • | • | • | | | • | | • | 4.0/5

IMPERIAL OAK BREWING

PRO TIPS

» Dog friendly on the patio only.

» No kitchen, but offers a full bar, replete with cider, liquor, wine, and cyser options.

» There's some table seating inside, but if the weather's nice, there's no reason for you to not be out on their large sunny patio.

» Plenty of food trucks come by on Friday, Saturday, and Sunday, but it's always best to check in advance.

» For the nature and cycling lover, the location is a dream, adjacent to the Des Plaines River and the Illinois Centennial Trail. If you have a day to kill, and a decent bike, this is an ideal way to spend your time.

Terry Hamilton

DATE OF VISIT:

MY RATING
☆ ☆ ☆ ☆ ☆

NOTES:

POPULAR BEERS

| Predic-tion... Pain? | Crank It Hop | Udderly Black | Quiet Giant |

M	Tu	W	Th	F	S	Su
12-11p	12-11p	12-11p	12p-12a	12p-1a	11a-1a	11a-11p

ITASCA BREWING COMPANY

FIELD NOTES

400 E. Orchard St.
Itasca, IL 60143
630-773-1800
itascabrewingcom-pany.com

While they've been brewing since 2011, early in 2017 Itasca Brewing decided to call Itasca Country Club their home. Open to the public, guests are not required to have a membership in order to enjoy some refreshing beers (sorry, no golf is included). Despite the small space, there are still quite a few options for every beer lover's enjoyment, including an adjacent restaurant for hungry drinkers. With the fermentation tanks directly behind the bar, no need for a brewery tour - you're sitting in it.

OWNER
Not provided

DATE FOUNDED
2011

HEAD BREWER
Michael Valente

AVAILABILITY
Taproom only

BEST KNOWN FOR
English styles, pales

| 14 | 100 | | | • | • | | | • | | 3.7/5 |

ITASCA BREWING COMPANY

PRO TIPS

» Make sure to call in advance. They do close often for private events. After all, it's a country club.

» A restaurant, Fox and Turtle, is located behind the taproom in case you are hungry - order directly while seated in the taproom.

» It is a country club, so sloppy attire could be an issue. Keep your favorite cut-off drinking shorts at home.

DATE OF VISIT:

MY RATING
☆ ☆ ☆ ☆ ☆

NOTES:

POPULAR BEERS

Citra Session Pale Ale

Bean Smith

M	Tu	W	Th	F	S	Su
closed	4-9p	4-9p	4-9p	4-10p	12-10p	1-4p

KINSLAHGER BREWING COMPANY

FIELD NOTES

6806 Roosevelt Rd.
Oak Park, IL 60304
844-552-4437
kinslahger.com

The Kinslahger taproom feels like a throwback to another era once you step inside. The space is stylish with dark brown hues and black and white photos. With its classic bar feel, it's easy to see why it's become a neighborhood staple. KInslahger maximizes its small space creating a classy room of cozy comfort. The name Kinslahger is a mash-up of three things: Kinship (connection of individuals), lager (their focus beer) and the first letter of the last name of each of the three owners.

OWNER
Steve Loranz, Neal Armstrong, Keith Huizinga

HEAD BREWER
Steve Loranz

AVAILABILITY
Chicago - limited

BEST KNOWN FOR
Lagers

DATE FOUNDED
2016

PUBLIC TRANSIT
'L' Blue/Oak Park

12	48			•		•			•	4.2/5

KINSLAHGER BREWING COMPANY

PRO TIPS

» Bring your own food or enjoy one of their artisanal snacks.

» It's a small space so be prepared for it to quickly get crowded on the weekend.

» While they tell you not to tip (multiple times), all tips get donated to the American Federation for Suicide Prevention! So still tip.

» No cash accepted, so bring your credit card.

» Two popular music venues, Fitzgerald's and Wire, are located down the street so get your pre-show drink here.

DATE OF VISIT:

MY RATING
☆☆☆☆☆

NOTES:

POPULAR BEERS

   Dunkel

M	Tu	W	Th	F	S	Su
closed	closed	3-10p	3-10p	3p-12a	11a-12a	12-5p

LUNAR BREWING CO.

FIELD NOTES

54 E. St. Charles Rd.
Villa Park, IL 60181
630-530-2077

Lunar is old-school. Some may call it a dive. Outside appearances might put off some potential newcomers. It's got wood-paneling, a darker sort of ambiance lit primarily by neon signs, and an overall outside impression that, if you're driving by, you could blink and you'll probably miss it. However, if you're looking for craft beer and a place that takes you to the look and feel of a Chicago bar from back in your grandparents' day, this long-running establishment is the place.

OWNER
Charlie Tierney

HEAD BREWER
Kevin Hopkins

AVAILABILITY
Taproom only

BEST KNOWN FOR
Variety

DATE FOUNDED
1996

2017 PRODUCTION
100 bbl

PUBLIC TRANSIT
UP-W/Villa Park

| 17 | 105 | | | • | | • | | • | 3.9/5 |

LUNAR BREWING CO.

PRO TIPS

» More of a "local watering hole" than a "brewpub," and for that reason it should be loved and treasured.

» Beers are made on a very small scale. Real small. They're brewed in soup kettles. So, every batch is rare and exclusive.

» The owner has been known to sit at the bar and socialize with guests, so feel free to introduce yourself.

» No website (really old school), so don't try to get their latest draft list online.

» Very friendly regulars - be sure to strike up a conversation.

DATE OF VISIT:

MY RATING
☆ ☆ ☆ ☆ ☆

NOTES:

POPULAR BEERS

Moon-dance IPA	Raspber-ry Cream	Total Eclipse Stout	Neil Arm-strong

M	Tu	W	Th	F	S	Su
12p-1a	12p-1a	12p-1a	12p-1a	12p-2a	12p-2a	12p-1a

MISKATONIC BREWING COMPANY

FIELD NOTES

1000 N. Frontage Rd.
Darien, IL 60561
630-541-9414
**miskatonicbrewing.
com**

If the works of horror fiction writer H.P. Lovecraft inspired you to start a brewery, these folks beat you to it (Miskatonic was the name of a fictional university in Lovecraftian lore). Miskatonic is the collective creation of a couple alums from Chicago area's best-known breweries. Brewery manager and co-founder Josh Mowry arrives from Two Brothers, while head brewer John Wyskiewicz used to ply his trade at Gordon Biersch and Goose Island. Together, they craft unique brews that recreate classic and well-loved styles.

OWNER
Josh Mowry, John Wyzkiewicz

HEAD BREWER
John Wyzkiewicz

AVAILABILITY
Chicago, OH

BEST KNOWN FOR
IPAs, pales, English styles, saisons, barrel aging and mixed fermentation

DATE FOUNDED
2015

KEY EVENTS
Anniversary Party (Jul)

14 | 115 | • | • | • | | • | | • | | 4.0/5

MISKATONIC BREWING COMPANY

PRO TIPS

- » Bright, cinder block tasting room with a copper-clad bar.
- » Occasionally features food trucks, or just bring your own food.
- » Free tours every Sunday at 3pm.
- » Plenty of board game options are available in the taproom for those inclined. Trivia night happens on a fairly regular basis, usually on Wednesdays.
- » Recently added a private event space and live music.
- » Credit card only; they don't accept cash.
- » Fun fact: taproom manager AJ Blume is also an award-winning affineur (someone that ages cheeses until they're ready to eat).

POPULAR BEERS

DATE OF VISIT:

MY RATING
☆ ☆ ☆ ☆ ☆

NOTES:

M	Tu	W	Th	F	S	Su
closed	3-10p	3-10p	3-10p	3-11p	12-11p	12-7p

MORE BREWING CO.

FIELD NOTES

126 S. Villa Ave.
Villa Park, IL 60181
630-501-1519
morebrewing.com

Owners Sunny and Perry Patel are serial entrepreneurs who arrived in the US as teenagers and prove that the American dream is still alive. They struck gold for MORE when they nabbed Shaun Berns, a brewmaster with a sterling reputation. Berns cut his teeth at the RAM Schaumburg brewpub and built a passionate following for his IPAs and other brews. These fans now flock to MORE for special releases, joined by the throngs who learned about MORE after their impressive Best in Show win at the 2017 FOBAB festival.

OWNER
Sunny Patel, Perry Patel

HEAD BREWER
Shaun Berns

AVAILABILITY
Brewpub only

BEST KNOWN FOR
Imperial stouts, NE IPAs, fruit beers

DATE FOUNDED
2017

KEY AWARDS
FoBAB 2017 (2)

16 | 300 | | | • | • | | • | | | 4.2/5

MORE BREWING CO.

PRO TIPS

» The dining area at MORE abuts against the brewing setup, giving guests a great view of the brite tanks. It's a large space with plenty of seating, and impressive-looking MORE branded chairs.

» While there's parking in nearby lots, if you're into cycling, MORE is right off the Prairie Path, an east-west bike path that starts in Forest Park and goes all the way (in three different branches) to Aurora, Geneva and Elgin.

» The menu is upscale pub food with some terrific food & drink specials on Mondays and Tuesdays.

» Keep an eye out for bottle releases at the brewpub and if Henna Imperial Stout is on draft, do not miss.

DATE OF VISIT:

MY RATING
☆ ☆ ☆ ☆ ☆

NOTES:

POPULAR BEERS

| Henna | Loose Candies | Dusty | Frooted Beer Series |

M	Tu	W	Th	F	S	Su
11a-11p	11a-11p	11a-11p	11a-11p	11a-12a	11a-12a	1030-11

MYTHS AND LEGENDS BREWING CO.

FIELD NOTES

Myths and Legends Brewing began in 2013 as Urban Legend, with the concept that all of their beers would be named after famed legends and tales of the recent (and sometimes, distant) past. The brewery changed its name to Myths and Legends in 2016, but has continued to stick with its tried-and-true M.O. of producing a well-tuned mix of sessionable brews and bigger, imperial beers for the more enthusiastic drinker.

1115 Zygmunt Cir.
Westmont, IL 60559
630-442-7864
mythsandlegends-beer.com

OWNER
Jason Hancock,
Andrew Matt, Tom
Budreck, Bob
Behrens, Shannon
Hancock

HEAD BREWER
David Leeds

AVAILABILITY
Chicago

BEST KNOWN FOR
Pales, imperial ales

DATE FOUNDED
2013

KEY EVENTS
Summer Party (Jun),
Legends of the Fall
(Sept), Day of the
Dead (Oct)

10 | 40 | | • | • | • | | | • | | 3.8/5

MYTHS AND LEGENDS BREWING CO.

PRO TIPS

» Occupies a space in an otherwise nondescript modern-yet-industrial looking building that could be mistaken anywhere else for an anonymous warehouse.

» Though there isn't much seating at the bar, there are plenty of tables to sit at, barrels to stand around, and even a couple of couches in the corner for those feeling a bit more sedentary.

» Has a "Legends Club," which, for a small fee, allows members first crack at reserving barrel-aged and other special release bottles, a pass to their annual summer and taproom anniversary parties, a logo'd pint glass, and a small discount in the merchandise shop.

» Live music on Wed. and Thur.

DATE OF VISIT:

MY RATING
☆ ☆ ☆ ☆ ☆

NOTES:

POPULAR BEERS

| The Creature | Cooper's Parachute | Catherine The Great | Scylla's Grasp |

M	Tu	W	Th	F	S	Su
closed	5-10p	5-10p	5-10p	3p-12a	12p-12a	12-8p

NOON WHISTLE BREWING

FIELD NOTES

800 E. Roosevelt Rd.
Lombard, IL 60148
630-376-6895
**noonwhistlebrewing.
com**

Usually it takes an extreme amount of hops or alcohol for a brewery to gain some buzz around craft beer circles. However, in 2014 Noon Whistle came into the beer scene looking to flip that script, with a remarkably consistent stream of sessionable brews that always seem to impress. Since then, they have ventured into some higher ABV offerings and they've quickly become known for their hazy IPAs as well as the Smack series of sours that are great for enthusiasts of approachably tart beers.

OWNER
Paul Kreiner, Mike Condon, Jim Cagle

HEAD BREWER
Paul Kreiner

AVAILABILITY
Chicago

BEST KNOWN FOR
Session ales, sours, NE IPAs

DATE FOUNDED
2014

2017 PRODUCTION
1,900 bbl

11 | 80 | • | • | • | • | | • | | 4.0/5

NOON WHISTLE BREWING

PRO TIPS

» There's no kitchen, but you can bring your own food. Food trucks are featured on Fridays.

» Go for one of their popular Gummy beers but make sure you try a sour or a sessionable before you leave.

» Their parking lot is shared with an adjacent Whirlyball (a game that mixes jai alai, basketball, and bumper cars). Just make sure to drink session ales before piloting a bumper car around.

» Full size drafts are $4 all day on Tuesday, $1 off on Wednesday, and growler deals on Thursday.

» Ask to see their removable-lid beer cans. With a bigger opening, you'll get a lot more aroma when drinking from the can!

POPULAR BEERS

| Gummy Series | Smack Sour Series | Hop Prizm Series | Cozmo |

DATE OF VISIT:

MY RATING
☆ ☆ ☆ ☆ ☆

NOTES:

M	Tu	W	Th	F	S	Su
closed	12-10p	12-10p	12-10p	12-11p	12-11p	12-7p

OAK PARK BREWING COMPANY

FIELD NOTES

155 S. Oak Park Ave.
Oak Park, IL 60302
708-445-0272
oakparkbeer.com

Oak Park was another longtime-dry suburb of Chicago (see also: Wheaton & Evanston), opening itself back up to alcohol sales in 1972. But, it took another 40+ years for its first brewery to open. Oak Park is a sister project of the Hamburger Mary's team, so expect a couple of shared beer recipes, more clever beer names, and the same sports bar with a ton of camp-atmosphere that you'll find at the Andersonville mainstay. As a friendly, neighborhood brewpub that just might happen to have a drag show going on next door, this unique business is filling a need in Oak Park.

OWNER
Brandon Wright,
Ashley Wright, Jim
Cozzens

HEAD BREWER
Jim Cozzens

AVAILABILITY
Brewpub only

BEST KNOWN FOR
Pales, Belgians,
lagers

DATE FOUNDED
2016

2017 PRODUCTION
350 bbl

PUBLIC TRANSIT
'L' Green/Oak Park

| 14 | 100 | • | | • | • | | • | | • | 3.4/5 |

OAK PARK BREWING COMPANY

PRO TIPS

» Much like Hamburger Mary's, there's seating at the bar, with plenty of tables, booths, nooks, and hodgepodge decorations.

» The entrance has a British-style police call box familiar to fans of the TV series Doctor Who.

» The pub grub available here is a bit different from Hamburger Mary's, with spent grain flatbreads and veggie burgers featuring the brewery's used husks.

» HamBINGO Mary's is every Tuesday night and Sunday, trivia night is every Wednesday, and comedy night is every Thursday. Friday and Saturday evenings feature Dining with the Divas, a dinner-and-drag show, Mary-oke (karaoke).

POPULAR BEERS

Frank Lloyd Rye IPA	Speak-easy Saison	Helles Other People

DATE OF VISIT:

MY RATING

NOTES:

M	Tu	W	Th	F	S	Su
4-10p	4-10p	4-10p	4-10p	4p-12a	11a-12a	11a-12a

SHORT FUSE BREWING

FIELD NOTES

On the southeast edge of O'Hare Airport, Schiller Park's Short Fuse Brewing isn't far from the Allstate Arena and the downtown Rosemont craziness of hotels, outlet malls, chain restaurants and the convention center. Opened in June of 2017, Short Fuse combines an approachability that you would expect for a brewery that serves such a wide-ranging crowd of visitors and tourists, with enough adventurous experiments to keep things interesting for the locals.

5000 N. River Rd.
Schiller Park, IL 60176
847-260-5044
shortfusebrewing.com

OWNER
Nick Teague, Mark Duchow

DATE FOUNDED
2017

HEAD BREWER
Mark Duchow

AVAILABILITY
Chicagoland

BEST KNOWN FOR
IPAs, NE IPAs, stouts

14 | 225 | | | • | • | | • | • | | 3.5/5

SHORT FUSE BREWING

PRO TIPS

» The brewpub is a big space with an incredibly long bar that contains more 50 stools. Bartenders get a workout.

» Large garage doors open for the summer.

» A wide range of pizzas, burgers, sandwiches and salads are on the upscale pub menu. Beer is used in the preparation of several items including their nacho beer cheese sauce, the house "Beer BQ" sauce, and the honey glaze that's drizzled atop several dishes.

» Live music on Thursday, Friday and Saturday.

» Short Fuse has flight holders that can carry small pours of all 14 beers on tap.

DATE OF VISIT:

MY RATING

☆ ☆ ☆ ☆ ☆

NOTES:

POPULAR BEERS

M	Tu	W	Th	F	S	Su
closed	11a-10p	11a-10p	11a-11p	11a-11p	11a-11p	11a-9p

SKELETON KEY BREWERY

FIELD NOTES

8102 Lemont Rd.
Woodridge, IL 60517
630-395-9033
skeletonkeybrewery.com

Skeleton Key aims to be a neighborhood community hub, and an incubator of sorts for potential brewers. They offer a program called "Spare Keys," which, for the ambitious but hesitant homebrewer looking to start their own new brewery project, is a 12-week immersion program going through all the nitty gritty in running a production brewery. Consideration for the program is done through Skeleton Key's homebrew contest, the finalists of which may qualify for the Spare Keys program. They even offer to contract brew the winning beer for the program participant.

OWNER
Emily Slayton, Paul Slayton, John Szopa

HEAD BREWER
John Szopa

AVAILABILITY
Chicago - very limited

BEST KNOWN FOR
Pales, IPAs, dark ales, witbiers

DATE FOUNDED
2016

2017 PRODUCTION
320 bbl

KEY EVENTS
Anniversary Party/ Halloween Bash (Oct)

8 | 70 | | | • | | • | | • | | 4.0/5

SKELETON KEY BREWERY

PRO TIPS

» Skeleton Key's not just here to sell beer, they want to educate, too. Book a beer education class in advance (they sell out quickly) to learn about topics like Belgian styles and becoming a beer judge.

» Two separate bar-like seating areas can accommodate as many as 20, with tables and barrels for the rest of the crowd.

» Look for food trucks on the weekends.

» One tap at the taproom is reserved for experimental beers that are only available to members of Skeleton Key's Skullmuggery Society. Members get to drink out of skull-shaped glassware and drink the special beer. Reservations to that exclusive group become available every month.

DWL Images

DATE OF VISIT:

MY RATING
☆ ☆ ☆ ☆ ☆

NOTES:

POPULAR BEERS

| Friends Don't Lie | Migra-tory | Snuffed Out | Captain Tragedy |

M	Tu	W	Th	F	S	Su
closed	closed	4-10p	4-10p	3-11p	12-11p	12-6p

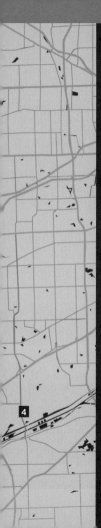

SUBURBS FAR WEST

NEIGHBORHOOD HIGHLIGHTS

BBGB BREWERY & HOP FARM

FIELD NOTES

2000 W. Orchard Rd.
North Aurora, IL 60542
630-299-3977
eathardware.com

Sustainability practices are the name of the game for BBGB, with spent grain from the brewery being used for the restaurant's pizza dough, dinner rolls, slider buns, and dog treats. Decor and architecture is all reused/recycled/salvaged (railroad ties, re-purposed glass, whiskey barrels, etc.). There's also a green wall at the entrance, regulating temperature for the building, and providing a lovely, almost rainforest sort of vibe on the outside of this suburban destination. The plan is to have the 1.5-acre hop farm generate 80% of the brewery's hops.

OWNER
Bruce Burns, Brent Fiedor

HEAD BREWER
Brent Fiedor

AVAILABILITY
Chicago - limited draft only

BEST KNOWN FOR
IPAs, saisons, dark ales

DATE FOUNDED
2016

| 20 | 210 | • | | • | | | • | • | | 3.5/5 |

BBGB BREWERY & HOP FARM

PRO TIPS

» Brewery tours do not need to be scheduled, but rather a friendly manager or brewer can take your group on a tour with a simple ask.

» Tours feature not just the brewery, but also the hop farm, greenhouse, and other sustainability practices that BBGB undertakes.

» Most meats are smoked and cured in-house too, featuring a brisket hot dog and charcuterie plates of various sizes.

» Food from Hardware (the name of the restaurant adjacent to the taproom) can be ordered in the taproom.

» For fans of brown liquor, Hardware offers over 350 whiskey selections.

DATE OF VISIT:

MY RATING
☆ ☆ ☆ ☆ ☆

NOTES:

POPULAR BEERS

Earl The Pearl	Barney's Coffee Stout	Butch's Badass Porter

M	Tu	W	Th	F	S	Su
closed	11a-10p	11a-10p	11a-10p	11a-12a	11a-12a	12-9p

DRY CITY BREW WORKS

FIELD NOTES

120 N. Main St.
Wheaton, IL 60187
630-456-4787
**drycitybrewworks.
com**

With over 70 churches in the area, plus the presence of evangelical Wheaton College, Wheaton is regarded as one of Chicago's more conservative suburbs. There's even a rumor that the 80s film Footloose was based on the small city. Liquor sales in restaurants weren't opened up until 1985, but the craft beer boom has led to this suburb opening up a brewpub. Dry City plays on this history, not only in its name, but in the speakeasy-esque side entrance to the taproom itself. While Dry City could get by merely on its back-story, they take their beer seriously too.

OWNER
Ben Sampson,
Jessica Sampson,
David Carr, Lori Carr

HEAD BREWER
Ben Sampson

AVAILABILITY
Taproom and limited
local restaurants

BEST KNOWN FOR
Stouts, red ales

DATE FOUNDED
2014

PUBLIC TRANSIT
UP-W/Wheaton

8 | 70 | • | • | • | | • | | • | • | 4.0/5

DRY CITY BREW WORKS

PRO TIPS

» Located on a quaint main street in an area that screams small-town Midwestern America, this classy taproom sports exposed brick and classy, wooden furniture that helps to modernize, but also shouts out the past of the building. Edison bulbs hang above, and pressed tin tiles are tacked underneath the bar.

» Greatly expanded their space this last year, but maintained their speakeasy side entrance and cool outdoor patio.

» Only permits 3 servings (1 serving = 1 pint or flight) of alcohol per person per day, so plan accordingly.

» Local musicians play on Fridays and Saturdays.

» Credit cards only.

DATE OF VISIT:

MY RATING
☆ ☆ ☆ ☆ ☆

NOTES:

POPULAR BEERS

Provi- dence Coff. Milk Stout	Light as the Breeze	Baby's Toupee	I Saved The King Scotch Ale

M	Tu	W	Th	F	S	Su
closed	closed	4-9p	4-9p	3-10p	2-10p	2-6p

HOPVINE BREWING CO.

FIELD NOTES

4030 Fox Valley
Center Dr.
Aurora, IL 60504
630-229-6030
**hopvinebrewing-
company.com**

Opened in October 2013, Hopvine is located in an a strip mall close to the Fox Valley Mall and just a short drive from the famous Aurora Outlet Mall. Husband and wife team, Jan and Doug Isley, had previously worked in the beer industry before opening up Hopvine. It's a family-run business and focuses on craft beer as well as an extensive food menu. While they have a long bar that is great if you want to grab a quick drink, if you want to settle down, order some food and listen to the live music they have on the weekends they also have a large area with tables.

OWNER
Doug Isley, Jan Isley

DATE FOUNDED
2013

HEAD BREWER
Ken McMullen

AVAILABILITY
Limited local draft
only

BEST KNOWN FOR
Wheat ales, red/
brown ales

32 | 277 | • | | | • | • | | | • | • | | 3.5/5

HOPVINE BREWING CO.

PRO TIPS

» They have a big menu that features sandwiches, wraps, and small plates.

» Chef driven food made from scratch creates a unique intimacy between their beer and menu selections. They have their own garden and even grow some hops.

» Always have two craft sodas available.

» Live music on Saturdays - it can get loud so if you prefer a quiet setting, go before the music.

» Happy hour is from 4-7p everyday they are open.

DATE OF VISIT:

MY RATING
☆ ☆ ☆ ☆ ☆

NOTES:

POPULAR BEERS

Brew Monkey	Urban Tumble-weed	Mast-odon	Aurora Amber Ale

M	Tu	W	Th	F	S	Su
closed	4-10p	4-10p	11a-11p	11a-12a	11a-12a	11a-9p

METAL MONKEY BREWING

FIELD NOTES

515 Anderson Dr.
Romeoville, IL 60446
815-524-3139
**metalmonkeybrew-
ing.com**

The people behind the simian-flashing-
devil-horns logo of Metal Monkey are
self-starters. Brandi Camp styles herself
as the owner and ringmaster, while Dan
Camp and Jason Janes are the head
brewers. The three founders did much
of Metal Monkey's buildout on their
own. Though they admit the operation
isn't the fanciest in the world, they more
than make up for it with their beer. The
brewing system is only three barrels
(93 gallons), which means that there's
always plenty of beer turnover at the
90-seat taproom.

OWNER
Dan Camp, Brandi
Camp, Jason Janes

HEAD BREWER
Dan Camp, Jason
Janes

AVAILABILITY
Very limited - draft
only

BEST KNOWN FOR
Sours, stouts, hop
forward varieties

DATE FOUNDED
2016

2017 PRODUCTION
400 bbl

KEY EVENTS
Bourbon Barrel-
Aged Asmodeus
bottle release
(winter)

16 | 90 | | | • | • | | | | • | | 4.0/5

METAL MONKEY BREWING

PRO TIPS

» Metal Monkey is laid-back, comfortable and welcoming to all. You get a good look into their ethos when you see their house rules (e.g. "Don't be a dick" and "No Hate" among others).

» There's plenty of seating to be had, at the bar, in the lounge, at small tables or at the community table - good for solo visits or 15 of your friends.

» Plenty of board games available for patrons to enjoy while having their brews.

» Don't forget trivia on Mondays and food trucks on the weekends.

» Discounts available if you're a first responder, military personnel or teacher.

DATE OF VISIT:

MY RATING
☆ ☆ ☆ ☆ ☆

NOTES:

POPULAR BEERS

| Fonkey Mucker | Tony's Car | Simian Fever | Asmo-deus |

M	Tu	W	Th	F	S	Su
12-9p	closed	closed	12-9p	12-11p	12-11p	12-9p

MIDNIGHT PIG BEER

FIELD NOTES

12337 South Rte 59
Plainfield, IL 60585
815-436-3900
nevinsdraftco.com

A lot of breweries tout their game when it comes to being sustainable or green, and not in the Kermit the Frog way. Midnight Pig boasts of the brewery's donation of its spent grain to local farmers, not just for feed use, but also for composting and soil enrichment. The steaks, burgers, salads, and sides all benefit from this sort of circle of life. Like many other suburban destinations, you'll find some styles for craft beer initiates, including a pilsner, a Märzen, a Belgian witbier, and a pale ale, but you can also find a caramelly rich doppelbock, an imperial IPA, and an imperial red.

OWNER
Nevin's Restaurant Group

HEAD BREWER
N/A

AVAILABILITY
Limited draft only

BEST KNOWN FOR
Stouts, Belgians, lagers

DATE FOUNDED
2013

2017 PRODUCTION
560 bbl

RECENT AWARDS
GABF 2016

20 | 300 | • | | • | • | | • | • | | 3.1/5

MIDNIGHT PIG BEER

PRO TIPS

- » Nevin's Brewing Company is still the name of this brewpub, but they recently rebranded their beer to Midnight Pig Beer.
- » They boast perhaps the most encyclopedic wing menu of any brewpub in the city, featuring bone-in, boneless, and tenders options, plus your choice of over a dozen different sauces.
- » Features local live music (sometimes with a cover) on most weekend nights.
- » Hosts a trivia night on most Wednesdays.
- » Food and drink specials on Sundays and Tuesday to Thursday.
- » When there's a big game on, they'll have it on at the taproom.

POPULAR BEERS

Hook & Hatchet	Apoca-lyptina-tor	Pinched IPA	Boot-leggers Paradise

M	Tu	W	Th	F	S	Su
closed	3p-12a	3p-12a	3p-12a	3p-2a	11:30-2	11:30-11

DATE OF VISIT:

MY RATING
☆ ☆ ☆ ☆ ☆

NOTES:

PENROSE BREWING COMPANY

FIELD NOTES

Head Brewer Tom Korder founded Penrose after his departure from Goose Island in 2013. Penrose is known for producing Belgian-inspired session ales, oak-fermented wild ales and fresh hop flavors. Expect a wide variety of draft offerings at any given time when you visit the taproom. It's obvious that Korder loves working with various flavors, fermenting organisms, and aging methods with his beers. He gives them the time they need and the results are justification for the time and effort spent.

509 Stevens St.
Geneva, IL 60134
630-232-2115
**penrosebrewing.
com**

OWNER	DATE FOUNDED
Tom Korder	2014
HEAD BREWER	KEY EVENTS
Tom Korder	Bottle releases for wild series; Funk Beer Festival (Sep)
AVAILABILITY	
IL	
	PUBLIC TRANSIT
BEST KNOWN FOR	UP-W/Geneva
Belgians, sours, pales, IPAs	

15 | 105 | | | | • | | | | • | | • | 3.9/5

PENROSE BREWING COMPANY

PRO TIPS

» Bottle releases usually generate sizable lines, so if you're headed to one of these, make sure you dress for the weather and allow yourself plenty of time.

» Expect plenty of variety and a special beer or two on tap any time you go. Many of their beers don't get distribution. You can only try them at the taproom or by filling up your growler.

» Penrose's "Ten Buck Tour" gets you a beer and a glass you can keep; tours are available Friday, Saturday, and Sunday, and can be booked online.

» Taproom is credit card only.

» Food trucks will show up periodically, but you can also bring your own food.

DATE OF VISIT:

MY RATING
☆ ☆ ☆ ☆ ☆

NOTES:

POPULAR BEERS

M	Tu	W	Th	F	S	Su
1-9p	1-9p	1-9p	1-9p	1-10p	11a-10p	11a-6p

SOLEMN OATH BREWERY

FIELD NOTES

1661 Quincy Ave.
Naperville, IL 60540
630-995-3062
**solemnoathbrewery.
com**

Heavy metal imagery and intimidating label art (including beer names like Pain Cave, Wreckage Master, Death by Viking, and Punk Rock for Rich Kids) obscures the delicious and drinkable brews of this Naperville brewery. Brothers John and Joe Barley (what a great last name for a brewer) opened Solemn Oath in 2012 after hosting a tasting with friends. Their focus is on West Coast, Belgian, and barrel-aged beers, but that doesn't stop them from making a mean Kölsch (Lü), or experimenting with other styles.

OWNER
John Barley

HEAD BREWER
Andrew Mason

AVAILABILITY
Chicago, WI

BEST KNOWN FOR
IPAs, hoppy reds,
Belgians, Kölsch

DATE FOUNDED
2012

RECENT AWARDS
GABF 2016

KEY EVENTS
Oath Day (Jun)

14 | 132 | • | | • | | | | • | | 3.9/5

SOLEMN OATH BREWERY

PRO TIPS

» A half wall divides the brewing quarters from the taproom space, allowing guests the chance to see the process in all its glory.

» The "Oath Day" anniversary party every June is a large affair featuring food trucks, out-of-rotation beers, and general mayhem.

» Three beer limit per day (local law).

» The Old Order club is a great way to get access to exclusive events, beer releases and a lot more. Cost for 2017 was $195.

» Recently expanded the taproom footprint and added an outdoor German-style beer garden.

» Credit card only and no tips.

DATE OF VISIT:

MY RATING
☆ ☆ ☆ ☆ ☆

NOTES:

POPULAR BEERS

M	Tu	W	Th	F	S	Su
12-9p	12-9p	12-9p	12-9p	12-11p	11a-11p	11a-7p

TWO BROTHERS ARTISAN BREWING

FIELD NOTES

30W315 Calumet Ave. W
Warrenville, IL 60555
630-393-2337
**twobrothersbrewing.
com**

Launched in 1996 by Jim and Jason
Ebel, the original location for Two
Brothers is a Warrenville warehouse
and the spot we chose to feature
(after all, it's the granddaddy). Today,
Two Brothers maintains four spaces
in the Chicago area as well as one in
Scottsdale, Arizona. The Roundhouse
in Aurora, formerly owned by Walter
Payton, features a huge outdoor garden.
A third spot in Naperville called The
Craftsman is a gastropub and cocktail
bar. The Social Tap opened in downtown
Oak Park highlights favorites of the
other locations. Each is an excellent pick
for sampling beers that have impressed
Chicagoans for 21 years running.

OWNER
Jim Ebel, Jason Ebel

HEAD BREWER
Alex Makowski

AVAILABILITY
IL, IN, AZ, FL, CT,
NJ, IA, OH, MD, MO,
TN, WI

BEST KNOWN FOR
Pales, IPAs,
Belgians, sours

DATE FOUNDED
1996

2017 PRODUCTION
40,000 bbl

RECENT AWARDS
GABF 2016, WBC
2016, FoBAB 2016

KEY EVENTS
Oktoberfest (Sep),
Summer Festival
(Jun)

18 | 250 | • | | • | • | | • | • | | 3.7/5

TWO BROTHERS ARTISAN BREWING

PRO TIPS

» Visit their other locations at: 205 N. Broadway, Aurora, IL; 100 S. Marion St., Oak Park, IL; 16 W. Jefferson, Naperville, IL.

» The Warrenville Tap House has more of a standard suburban brewpub atmosphere. Do a brewery tour on Saturday or Sunday afternoon.

» You'll always something unique, rare or barrel-aged in Warrenville as four of their draft lines are dedicated to their Special Projects division.

» The Roundhouse is a former 1856 railway building that is impressive in itself. In addition to the outdoor garden, there's also a music venue. It's also a popular spot for a wide variety of private events including weddings.

POPULAR BEERS

DATE OF VISIT:

MY RATING
☆ ☆ ☆ ☆ ☆

NOTES:

M	Tu	W	Th	F	S	Su
11a-11p	11a-11p	11a-11p	11a-11p	11a-12a	11a-12a	11a-9p

WERK FORCE BREWING CO.

FIELD NOTES

14903 S. Center St.
Plainfield, IL 60544
815-531-5557
**werkforcebrewing.
com**

This nanobrewery in Plainfield makes use of the resources available at its sister homebrew shop, Chicago Brew Werks, such as experimental ingredients and yeast strains to create continuously new and risky beers. Wild, sour, and fruit-infused beers are a main feature of Werk Force, which still doesn't eschew keeping a hoppy option and a stout on tap. With the entire resources of a massive homebrew store at their disposal, one can only feel like the brewers at Werk Force are children working at the candy store, or DJs working at the record store.

OWNER
Brandon Wright,
Amanda Wright

HEAD BREWER
Brandon Wright,
Steve Woertendyke,
Jake LaDuke, Jake
Scheufler

AVAILABILITY
Limited local

BEST KNOWN FOR
IPAs, pales, saisons

DATE FOUNDED
2014

RECENT AWARDS
FoBAB 2016, 2017

KEY EVENTS
Anniversary Party
(Jun)

24 | 100 | | | • | | • | | • | | • | | 4.3/5

WERK FORCE BREWING CO.

PRO TIPS

» Recently completed a huge expansion just a few doors down from the old space (in the same building). And they now have bar stools (and plenty of other seating).

» It's not often that you get a world-class homebrew shop (the largest in the Midwest) next to your taproom, so definitely check the Chicago Brew Werks store out and see if the homebrew bug bites you. And they still operate the 13 taps in this space for enjoyment while you shop.

» Note that the old space/homebrew shop is open Tue-Sun from morning to early evening.

» There's no kitchen, but food trucks will come by frequently.

DATE OF VISIT:

MY RATING
☆ ☆ ☆ ☆ ☆

NOTES:

POPULAR BEERS

The Beer Formerly Known As...	Oats Made Me Do It	Farm-house Vultures	Pressure Drop

M	Tu	W	Th	F	S	Su
closed	closed	closed	4-10p	4-10p	11a-10p	11a-7p

1. 350
2. Arrowhead
3. Blue Island
4. Evil Horse
5. Flossmoor Station
6. Hailstorm
7. One Trick Pony
8. Pollyanna
9. Rabid
10. Soundgrowler
11. Tribes

I-294
9
7

Hwy 1

4

NEIGHBORHOOD HIGHLIGHTS

1 Hollywood Casino Amphitheatre

2 Chicagoland Speedway

3 Original Rainbow Cone

4 Balmoral Racing Club

4

350 BREWING CO.

FIELD NOTES

350 was the street number of this brewing company's founders when they were undergraduates at Northern Illinois. Todd Randall and Erik Pizer (now head brewer at Rock Bottom in Warrenville, IL) were known to undertake dubious projects in their college days, including a nascent wrestling federation and punk bands based out of their attic. After Erik moved on to graduate school and Todd to a corporate job, the temptation for more crazy ideas continued until 2013 when they started 350 Brewing, likely one of their least dubious projects.

7144 183rd St.
Tinley Park, IL 60477
708-825-7339
350brewing.com

OWNER	**DATE FOUNDED**
Todd Randall	2013
HEAD BREWER	**KEY EVENTS**
Dusty Peters	350 Fest (Aug)
AVAILABILITY	
Taproom only	
BEST KNOWN FOR	
IPAs, lighter styles	

20 | 120 | | | • | • | | • | • | | 3.9/5

350 BREWING CO.

PRO TIPS

» August 2018 will mark the fourth iteration of 350 Fest, a brewery-run annual party hosted at the Tinley Park Convention Center. The festival combines 350's beer and punk and ska bands for a full day of mayhem and delight.

» The appetizer menu is filled with fried items, including wings, cheese sticks, fried dough, even avocado. Sandwiches include a burger, chicken, pot roast, BBQ pork, and an open-faced burger with fries slathered in cheese sauce called The Southside 'Shoe. Go big or go home.

» Very close to the Hollywood Casino Amphitheatre. Great place to go before or after a concert.

POPULAR BEERS

Crook County IPA	Howdy Neighbor	Stupid Kid	I Hate Mondays

M	Tu	W	Th	F	S	Su
12-10p	12-10p	12-10p	12-10p	12-12a	12-12a	12-8p

DATE OF VISIT:

MY RATING
☆ ☆ ☆ ☆ ☆

NOTES:

ARROWHEAD ALES BREWING COMPANY

FIELD NOTES

2101 Calistoga Dr.
New Lenox, IL 60451
815-717-6068
arrowheadales.com

New Lenox is closer to Joliet than it is to Chicago, but if you find yourself on the far southwestern side of the metro area, check out this 200-person restaurant/brewery. Founder and head brewer Mike Bacon's journey to craft beer is a well-trod story: sit in on some homebrewing sessions hosted by friends; research styles and the science behind making great beer; get homebrew set-up; hone your recipes; develop a pathological desire to share your creations with others; and voilà you can start a brewery. It's just that easy.

OWNER
Mike Bacon

HEAD BREWER
Mike Bacon

AVAILABILITY
Chicago - limited distribution

BEST KNOWN FOR
Stouts, IPAs

DATE FOUNDED
2016

PUBLIC TRANSIT
SWS/Laraway Rd.

12 | 200 | • | | • | • | | • | • | • | 3.8/5

ARROWHEAD ALES BREWING COMPANY

PRO TIPS

» Arrowhead's friendly suburban brick architecture houses an inviting atmosphere, and a spacious interior.

» For a suburban brewpub with the usual pizzas, appetizers, and burgers, there's a surprising level of experimentation with many options on the menu.

» The SMASH series features brews made with a single malt and single hop variety. It's a great way to explore the flavor capabilities of different component ingredients in beer.

» Live music is hosted several times each month, as well as Open Mic nights and beer education classes. Check Facebook posts for dates.

DATE OF VISIT:

MY RATING

NOTES:

POPULAR BEERS

| Devil's Breakfast | Weed Wacker | Coconut Killjoy | Entry Level Snob |

M	Tu	W	Th	F	S	Su
11a-10p	11a-10p	11a-10p	11a-10p	11a-1a	11a-1a	11a-10p

BLUE ISLAND BEER CO.

FIELD NOTES

13357 Old Western
Blue Island, IL 60406
708-954-8085
blueislandbeerco.com

Head brewer Bryan Shimkos has produced some truly great beers for a few different Chicago-area breweries, including Flossmoor Station and the now-defunct Ale Syndicate, before striking out on his own with this south suburban project just south of the Little Calumet River. His experiments with barrel-aging earned him a stellar reputation among those in-the-know with Chicago craft beer, and he brings that expertise to Blue Island. Expect a wide range of American-style beers with a healthy dose of IPAs and stouts.

OWNER
Bryan Shimkos, Alan Cromwell

HEAD BREWER
Bryan Shimkos

AVAILABILITY
Chicago

BEST KNOWN FOR
Stouts, IPAs, sessionable ales

DATE FOUNDED
2015

2017 PRODUCTION
550 bbl

KEY EVENTS
Uprising Craft Market (Apr, Dec)

PUBLIC TRANSIT
RI/Blue Island-Vermont, ME/Blue Island

12 | 56 | | • | • | • | • | | • | | • | 4.0/5

BLUE ISLAND BEER CO.

PRO TIPS

» Food trucks will be by occasionally, but you can also bring your own food. There are really good tacos and pizza right around the corner.

» One of the only taprooms with a few old-school arcade games.

» Expect a friendly, neighborhood crowd with a few dogs and many White Sox hoodies in attendance.

» Blue Island takes its music serious. Live performances on many weekends and a popular All Acoustic Bluegrass Jam the first Wednesday of the month.

DATE OF VISIT:

MY RATING
☆ ☆ ☆ ☆ ☆

NOTES:

POPULAR BEERS

M	Tu	W	Th	F	S	Su
closed	closed	4-10p	4-10p	4-10p	12-10p	12-6p

EVIL HORSE BREWING CO.

FIELD NOTES

1338 Main St.
Crete, IL 60417
708-304-2907
**evilhorsebrewing.
com**

In the far-south suburb of Crete you will find Evil Horse Brewing. Brewmaster Steve Kamp has been homebrewing since the 1980s, even serving as president of the Chicago Beer Society, a group of area beer enthusiasts that's been around as long as craft beer has been in Chicago. After receiving his education from Siebel and Doemens, and assisting at Brickstone, Flossmoor Station and Lagunitas, Kamp's got his own thing now. Sharing a name with his Evil Horse Farm, Kamp's beers represent a wide range of brewing styles from light lagers to barrel-aged stouts.

OWNER
Pinsetter Brands

HEAD BREWER
Steve Kamp

AVAILABILITY
IL

BEST KNOWN FOR
Pales, dark ales,
wheat ales

DATE FOUNDED
2015

KEY EVENTS
Anniversary Party
(Apr), Downtown
Hottie Days (Jun)

| 14 | 150 | • | • | • | • | | | • | | 3.8/5 |

EVIL HORSE BREWING CO.

PRO TIPS

» Remember the volcano in Iceland whose eruption in 2010 disrupted air travel all over Europe? Evil Horse named their Barrel-Aged Imperial Stout after it. It's called Eyjafjallajökull (AY-ya-FYAHD-la-JOO-kull-[tongue click]). You can also just call it "barrel-aged imperial stout" but it's up to you.

» The taproom mixes the atmosphere of an English pub with a small-town neighborhood gathering place.

» There's no kitchen at the taproom, but food trucks will come by occasionally.

» Brewery tours are on some Saturdays, but not all; call in advance.

» They're known for having fun events throughout the week like trivia, bingo and Euchre.

POPULAR BEERS

M	Tu	W	Th	F	S	Su
3-11p	3-11p	3-11p	3-11p	3p-12a	12p-12a	12-8p

DATE OF VISIT:

MY RATING
☆ ☆ ☆ ☆ ☆

NOTES:

FLOSSMOOR STATION

FIELD NOTES

1035 Sterling Ave.
Flossmoor, IL 60422
708-957-2739
**flossmoorstation.
com**

Quite possibly the first train station turned into a brewery in the Chicagoland area (beating out the roundhouse in Aurora that now carries the Two Brothers name). Flossmoor Station has been around since 1996, ancient by craft beer standards. But don't let their 20 years of experience fool you though. Flossmoor was named best small brewery in America at the 2006 Great American Beer Festival, and have continued to win prestigious awards for their beers since then, over 80 in total.

OWNER
Dean Armstrong,
Carolyn Armstrong

HEAD BREWER
Ryan Czaja

AVAILABILITY
Brewpub only

BEST KNOWN FOR
IPAs, brown/amber
ales, barrel-aged
beers

DATE FOUNDED
1996

KEY EVENTS
Pre-Dark Lord
Day (Apr/May),
Oktoberfest (Sept)

PUBLIC TRANSIT
ME/Flossmoor

16 | 240 | • | | • | • | | • | | • | 3.8/5

FLOSSMOOR STATION

PRO TIPS

» Though the brewpub is in an old, unused train station, across the street you'll find the Metra line that can take you directly north into downtown Chicago.

» Free happy hour buffet Friday 4-6p with a drink purchase.

» The woodgrain on the inside and outside gives a vibe somewhere between vintage train station, a German beer hall, and an upscale Midwestern family restaurant.

» Menu theme is "gourmet pub food," with sandwiches, BBQ, shared appetizers, and a cheese and charcuterie plate.

» Bombers of special releases are sometimes available at the brewery.

POPULAR BEERS

DATE OF VISIT:

MY RATING
☆ ☆ ☆ ☆ ☆

NOTES:

M	Tu	W	Th	F	S	Su
11:30-11	11:30-11	11:30-11	11:30-11	11:30-12	11:30-12	11:30-11

HAILSTORM BREWING CO.

FIELD NOTES

Since 2014, this Tinley Park brewery has gained fans for some of the most extreme beers made in the Chicago area. Their Vlad series of imperial stouts sees a massive number of permutations and reinterpretations with all sorts of adjuncts (coconut, raspberry, vanilla, etc.) and barrel-agings. They were one of the first Chicagoland breweries to try their hand at the hazy, buzzy New England-style IPA, which is known for not being too bitter, but heavily dry-hopped and left unfiltered for huge notes of orange juice and sweet citrus.

8060 W. 186th St.
Tinley Park, IL 60487
708-480-2268
hailstormbrewing.com

OWNER
Brandon Banbury,
Chris Schiller, Gene
Wabisczewicz, Josh
Wabisczewicz

HEAD BREWER
Brandon Banbury

AVAILABILITY
Chicago

BEST KNOWN FOR
NE IPAs, stouts

DATE FOUNDED
2014

RECENT AWARDS
FoBAB 2016, GABF
2015, 2017 (2)

KEY EVENTS
Anniversary Party
(Apr)

16 | 200 | | • | • | | | | • | | 4.2/5

HAILSTORM BREWING CO.

PRO TIPS

- » The Tasting Room shares a space with the impressively-sized production space, featuring barrels stacked as many as six high.
- » Go during nice weather if you want to get some natural light from the open garage door.
- » If you're looking for a session brew, this probably isn't your destination.
- » Close to 350, Soundgrowler and the Hollywood Casino Amphitheatre.
- » Open Mic Night on Thursdays. Live music, as well as food trucks on Fridays and Saturdays.
- » Don't pass on Prairie Madness if it's on tap. The IPA won the gold medal at the Great American Beer Festival in 2017, beating out 407 other IPAs.

POPULAR BEERS

M	Tu	W	Th	F	S	Su
closed	12-8p	12-8p	12-9p	12-10p	12-10p	12-8p

DATE OF VISIT:

MY RATING
☆ ☆ ☆ ☆ ☆

NOTES:

ONE TRICK PONY

FIELD NOTES

One Trick Pony

17933 Chappel Ave.
Lansing, IL 60438
708-889-6683
**onetrickponybrew-
ery.co**

With a mascot featuring a horse sporting a monstrously-toothy grin, One Trick Pony is one of those places that you don't have to worry if they're taking themselves too seriously or not. Out of the southern suburb of Lansing, their website is quick to level with the reader: "Our beer won't make you strong or handsome, but if you appreciate craft beer and want to meet some guys that are happy to make it, serve it, and probably drink it with you, stop by or give us a call." That sort of honesty is appreciated in craft beer these days.

OWNER
Mark Kocol

HEAD BREWER
Mark Kocol

AVAILABILITY
Chicago, NW IN

BEST KNOWN FOR
IPAs, red ales,
hefeweizens, stouts

DATE FOUNDED
2011

2017 PRODUCTION
700 bbl

24 | 50 | • | • | • | • | • | | • | | 4.1/5

ONE TRICK PONY

PRO TIPS

» The space is warm and inviting, with strings of exposed bulbs lighting the cinder block and wood-adorned space, letting you see their downright insane collection of vintage wooden beer boxes, growlers and other bottles lining the walls.

» During nice weather, the patio seating area is almost garden-like.

» Firkin Fridays let the taproom feature a cask-conditioned real ale to celebrate the end of the week.

» Bands will sometimes crowd into the corner to play live, but call in advance to see when the next artist is scheduled.

DATE OF VISIT:

MY RATING
☆ ☆ ☆ ☆ ☆

NOTES:

POPULAR BEERS

	Storm Cat	Warlander	Marsh Tacky

M	Tu	W	Th	F	S	Su
6-11p	3-11p	3-11p	3-11p	3-11p	3-11p	2-10p

POLLYANNA BREWING COMPANY

FIELD NOTES

POLLYANNA: a person characterized by irrepressible optimism with a tendency to find good in everything. Always seeing the glass as half full, the folks at Pollyanna folks believe optimism isn't just for foolish hearts, it's for the curious spirit. And they love sharing that optimistic approach with all beer drinkers. In 2017, Pollyanna opened their second location, "Roselare," in Roselle where it operates a brewery, taproom and "fermentarium" for one-off sours and wild beers. Now your curious and positive spirit can find even more to love about Pollyanna.

431 Talcott Ave.
Lemont, IL 60439
630-914-5834
pollyannabrewing. com

OWNER
Brian Pawola, Ed Malner, Paul Ciciora, Don Ciciora, Ryan Weidner

HEAD BREWER
Brian Pawola

AVAILABILITY
IL

BEST KNOWN FOR
IPAs, pales, lighter ales, Belgian, German, milk stouts

DATE FOUNDED
2013

2017 PRODUCTION
3,100 bbl

RECENT AWARDS
FoBAB 2017

KEY EVENTS
Berries & Bros (Apr), Beer Fest (Jun), Oktoberfest (Sept), Anniv. Party (Oct)

PUBLIC TRANSIT
HC/Lemont

| 12 | 46 | • | • | • | • | | • | • | 3.9/5 |

POLLYANNA BREWING COMPANY

PRO TIPS

» Visit their other location at: 245 E. Main Street, Roselle, IL.

» Dog friendly on the patio only.

» The taproom in Lemont is inviting, well-lit and stylish with about a dozen bar seats and some hi-top tables. Ample patio seating overlooking the historic I&M Canal is also available, weather permitting.

» The taproom in Roselle is a spacious open biergarten (inside and out) with many picnic tables and umbrellas.

» Tours are available during cold-weather months on Fridays and Saturdays with reservations available online.

» Generally live music on Fridays and food trucks on Saturdays, both locales.

POPULAR BEERS

DATE OF VISIT:

MY RATING
☆ ☆ ☆ ☆ ☆

NOTES:

M	Tu	W	Th	F	S	Su
closed	3-10p	3-10p	3-10p	3-11p	12-11p	12-7p

RABID BREWING

FIELD NOTES

Rabid Brewing is the first brewery in the southern suburb of Homewood. Like many local breweries, the husband and wife team split the duties of running the operation, with Cichon handling the brewing, which he'd been doing on an amateur level since 2011. Rabid focuses mainly on English-style beers with an American twist. Expect fantastic chalk art on the walls and live music on a regular basis.

17759 Bretz Dr.
Homewood, IL 60430
708-960-3193
rabidbrewing.com

OWNER
Tobias Cichon, Raiye Rosado

HEAD BREWER
Tobias Cichon

AVAILABILITY
Taproom only

BEST KNOWN FOR
IPAs, stouts

DATE FOUNDED
2017

KEY EVENTS
Anniversary (Oct)

10 | 100 | | | • | | | | • | 3.9/5

RABID BREWING

PRO TIPS

» Cichon is a writer with a passion for mythology which translates into fun beer names and even better beer descriptions on the menu.

» Rabid's taproom space is located behind a series of big box chain stores on Halsted Street, offering the opportunity to pick up any fast food option imaginable.

» Pair your visit with a stop at One Trick Pony, a direct shot 4 miles away.

» Open mic nights on Thursdays. Beer yoga on Sunday afternoons.

» Be sure to try one of their radler options as well.

DATE OF VISIT:

MY RATING
☆ ☆ ☆ ☆ ☆

NOTES:

POPULAR BEERS

M	Tu	W	Th	F	S	Su
closed	closed	4-10p	4-10p	4p-12a	4p-12a	3-9p

SOUNDGROWLER BREWING

FIELD NOTES

8201 183rd St. Ste P
Tinley Park, IL 60487
708-263-0083
soundgrowler.com

Sitting in an unassuming business park in Tinley Park, Soundgrowler is a heavy metal-themed brewery that's still friendly enough for bringing your parents and kids. The brewery opened in 2017 and features a nice array of sessionable and high-alcohol brews that operate in a surprisingly wide range of styles. The most popular beer is naturally, Orange Haze, their 7% ABV hazy IPA that hits all the right notes. With its high ceilings and striking black logo wall, the room feels large, open and welcoming. Hop forward beers, doom metal and tacos work quite well together.

OWNER	**DATE FOUNDED**
Arturo Lamas, Chris Pennington, Larry Hough	2017

HEAD BREWER
Larry Hough

AVAILABILITY
Chicago - limited

BEST KNOWN FOR
IPAs, pale ales, stouts

| 10 | 80 | | | • | | | • | • | | 4.1/5 |

SOUNDGROWLER BREWING

PRO TIPS

» Chances are, even at 11am on a Monday, you'll be hearing stoner metal (or some other metal subgenre) playing at a reasonable, suburban volume as you enter.

» A full menu of Mexican street food (tacos, burritos, tortas, nachos) is more than enough to satisfy your hunger, and pairs well with the beers.

» Pair with visits to Hailstorm and 350 Brewing, or before a concert at the Hollywood Casino Amphitheatre.

» Recently began offering bottle and can releases including a collaboration with Chicago sludge metal band Pale Horseman.

» Credit card only. No cash.

DATE OF VISIT:

MY RATING
☆ ☆ ☆ ☆ ☆

NOTES:

POPULAR BEERS

| Orange Haze | Grinder Punch | Riff Rider | Cave Dope |

M	Tu	W	Th	F	S	Su
11a-10p	11a-10p	11a-10p	11a-10p	11a-12a	11a-12a	12-8p

TRIBES BEER COMPANY

FIELD NOTES

11220 W. Lincoln Hwy
Mokena, IL 60448
815-464-0248
**tribesbeercompany.
com**

With locations in both Mokena and
Tinley Park, Tribes is quickly making
their mark on the brewpub scene in the
southwestern suburbs. Both locations
had been open as restaurants for quite
awhile (Mokena in 2009, Tinley Park in
2012) before the idea to start the Tribes
Beer Company came to fruition in 2015.
A 7-barrel system with six fermenters
allows for a decent amount of Tribes-
made beer to invade the taps at their
locations. The focus may be on hop-
forward brews, but that doesn't preclude
head brewer David Kerns from making
beers that are all over the map.

OWNER
Niall Freyne

DATE FOUNDED
2009

HEAD BREWER
Matt Voelker

2017 PRODUCTION
550 bbl

AVAILABILITY
IL - draft only

KEY EVENTS
Tribes Beer Fest
(Jul)

BEST KNOWN FOR
IPAs, pales, Kölsch

42 | 150 | • | | • | • | | • | • | | 3.7/5

TRIBES BEER COMPANY

PRO TIPS

» Visit their other locations at: 11120 Front St. Mokena, IL (taproom + beer garden); 9501 W. 171 St., Tinley Park, IL. (brewpub).

» The Mokena location features 38 different drafts while Tinley Park has 52 options. Check out their happy hour specials Monday to Friday.

» For food options, you can start by crafting your own meat and cheese plate, or getting some poutine of the day. Entrées and sandwiches are fairly by-the-book, but the Korean short rib tacos are good at any hour. New menu in 2018.

» Team trivia on Mondays and taco specials on Tuesdays.

» Close to the Hollywood Casino Amphitheater.

POPULAR BEERS

Daylight Kolsch	Craft'd IPA	Big Twin DIPA	Zero to 100 IIPA

DATE OF VISIT:

MY RATING

NOTES:

M	Tu	W	Th	F	S	Su
11:30-12	11:30-12	11:30-1a	11:30-1a	11:30-1a	11:30-1a	11:30-12

SUBURBS NORTHWEST INDIANA

1. 18th Street
2. 3 Floyds
3. Bulldog
4. Byway
5. The Devil's Trumpet
6. New Oberpfalz
7. Pokro
8. St. John Malt Brothers
9. Wildrose
10. Windmill

NEIGHBORHOOD HIGHLIGHTS

1. Gary SouthShore RailCats
2. Indiana Dunes National Lakeshore
3. Albanese Candy Factory
4. Horseshoe Hammond

18TH STREET BREWERY

FIELD NOTES

Drew Fox's career in craft beer started with a trip to Belgium more than a decade ago. After time spent at Pipeworks, Fox started brewing under the 18th Street name (the street in Chicago's Pilsen neighborhood where the idea for the brewery first came to Fox) via contract at Pipeworks and Spiteful. A successful Kickstarter campaign in 2012 led to the opening of a brewery and taproom in Gary, IN. Since then, a Hammond location has followed, as well as large amounts of well-deserved acclaim.

5417 Oakley Ave
Hammond, IN 46320
219-803-0820
18thstreetbrewery.com

OWNER
Drew Fox

HEAD BREWER
Drew Fox

AVAILABILITY
Chicago, NW IN

BEST KNOWN FOR
Imp. IPAs, pales, stouts

DATE FOUNDED
2012

RECENT AWARDS
FoBAB 2016

KEY EVENTS
Barrel Massacre
(varied dates)

12 | 200 | • | • | • | | | • | | 4.0/5

18TH STREET BREWERY

PRO TIPS

» Visit their other location at: 5725 Miller Ave, Gary, IN (the original location).

» Dog friendly on the patio at Hammond.

» Hammond will add an 18th Street Distillery tasting room in summer 2018.

» The Gary taproom has a smaller menu focused on perfect-for-lunch sandwiches and bar snacks. The Hammond brewpub's menu is larger.

» The rare barrel-aged bottle offering might be available, but be sure to check their regularly updated online list.

» Both locations have trivia nights and live entertainment, and Hammond has a giant outdoor bocce ball court.

POPULAR BEERS

M	Tu	W	Th	F	S	Su
11a-10p	11a-10p	11a-10p	11a-10p	11a-12a	11a-12a	11a-8p

DATE OF VISIT:

MY RATING
☆ ☆ ☆ ☆ ☆

NOTES:

3 FLOYDS BREWING CO.

FIELD NOTES

Founded in 1996, 3 Floyds is notorious for being rated as one of the Chicago area's best and most sought-after breweries. Their unassuming location, in a suburban office park still doesn't obscure that this metal-themed brewpub and brewery makes some serious beer in their own, idiosyncratic way. Nick Floyd/3 Floyds launched the first line of truly all hop-forward beer in the Midwest. They are also known for Dark Lord, a massive Russian Imperial Stout brewed with Dark Matter Coffee that is only available once a year during their ticketed event.

9750 Indiana Pkwy.
Munster, IN 46321
219-922-4425
3floyds.com

OWNER Nick Floyd	**DATE FOUNDED** 1996
HEAD BREWER Chris Boggess, Todd Haug	**RECENT AWARDS** WBC 2016
AVAILABILITY IL, IN, WI, OH, KY	**KEY EVENTS** Dark Lord Day (May)
BEST KNOWN FOR Pales, IPAs, imp. stouts	

20 | 75 | | | • | | | • | • | | 3.9/5

3 FLOYDS BREWING CO.

PRO TIPS

» The space is small, with metal music usually blaring. The place may seem intimidating or off-putting, even during a weekday lunch, but at the end of the day it's just a brewpub with excellent beers run by a bunch of metal-heads.

» The place's reputation precedes it, so expect a wait.

» There's a beer-to-go and a merch kiosk next to the pub. Perhaps you'll get lucky and be able to buy a case of Zombie Dust or a bottle of their latest barrel-aged release.

» As for the food, it's chef-driven pub fare with plenty to choose from, and nary a bum pick among the options.

» Recently launched collab brand with Mikkeller called WarPigs Brewing.

POPULAR BEERS

M	Tu	W	Th	F	S	Su
11a-12a	11a-12a	11a-12a	11a-12a	11a-12a	11a-12a	11a-12a

DATE OF VISIT:

MY RATING
☆ ☆ ☆ ☆ ☆

NOTES:

BULLDOG BREWING CO.

FIELD NOTES

1409 119th St.
Whiting, IN 46394
219-655-5284
**bulldogbrewingco.
com**

Brewmaster Kevin Clark and co-owner Jeff Kochis are both originally from northwest Indiana, and have come together to bring a welcoming, neighborhood brewpub to the small northwest Indiana city of Whiting. The blue-collar roots of Bulldog run deep with Clark as a steel worker and Kochis as a firefighter. This is the classic story of friends coming together over the love of homebrew and the ambition to have a brewery of one's own.

OWNER
Jeff Kochis, Kevin
Clark

HEAD BREWER
Kevin Clark

AVAILABILITY
NW IN

BEST KNOWN FOR
IPAs, classic
American styles

DATE FOUNDED
2011

20 | 100 | | | • | • | | • | | | 3.3/5

BULLDOG BREWING CO.

PRO TIPS

» A few guest drafts are available here, as is a full bar.

» Try some of the rarely-done styles that Clark puts together, like the Kentucky Common or almost-imperial-strength Bohemian lager.

» The wooden beams adorning the ceiling, and the occasional decorative surfboard, gives the brewpub a homey, unintimidating atmosphere.

» Bulldog's menu offers a bevy of sandwiches, burgers, pizza, pasta, and entrées.

» Thursdays feature a DJ and a raffle. Look for live bands during special brewpub events.

» Five minutes from Horseshoe Casino.

» Hit Whiting's Pierogi Fest in July.

POPULAR BEERS

DATE OF VISIT:

MY RATING
☆ ☆ ☆ ☆ ☆

NOTES:

M	Tu	W	Th	F	S	Su
11a-12a	11a-12a	11a-12a	11a-12a	11a-2a	11a-2a	11a-12a

BYWAY BREWING

FIELD NOTES

2825 Carlson Dr.
Hammond, IN 46323
219-844-5468
bywaybrewing.beer

Byway Brewing started off in the age old tradition of a bunch of seasoned home brewers and close friends coming together to brew beer. Fast forward to 2013, Dave Toth and Branko Sajn decided to turn that passion into a profession, creating a new destination brewpub in Hammond, IN, an easy jump off the busy I-94 corridor. David and Branko completed the brewpub in 2016 and have created a space where couples, families, and parties alike can enjoy amazing craft beer and food while escaping the buzz of the city.

OWNER
Dave Toth, Tom Duszynski, Branko Sajn

HEAD BREWER
Patrick Jones

AVAILABILITY
Chicago, NW IN

BEST KNOWN FOR
IPAs, porters, red ales

DATE FOUNDED
2016

RECENT AWARDS
IN Brewers Cup 2017

| 12 | 120 | • | | | • | • | | | • | | • | | 3.8/5 |

BYWAY BREWING

PRO TIPS

» Weekends get busy with private parties so if you can, try to visit during weekdays.

» Chef-driven menu. Try both the octopus and poutine appetizers; you won't be disappointed.

» Atmosphere includes soft rock music and three TVs that don't overwhelm the space (usually tuned to sports).

» Currently, almost all their beers are taproom only (with a few exceptions in town) so make sure to grab a growler or two before leaving.

» Right off the bike path. Make a stop here then continue riding to 3 Floyds.

DATE OF VISIT:

MY RATING
☆☆☆☆☆

NOTES:

POPULAR BEERS

M	Tu	W	Th	F	S	Su
11a-10p	11a-10p	11a-10p	11a-10p	11a-11p	11a-11p	11:30-9

THE DEVIL'S TRUMPET BREWING CO.

FIELD NOTES

8250 Utah St.
Merrillville, IN 46410
219-576-7118
thedevilstrumpet.com

Make sure to keep your GPS handy when trying to make your way to Merrillville, IN. But once there, you won't regret the journey. Heavy metal over the stereo, beers such as Make It A Cheeseburger IPA and the use of unique ingredients will definitely make this a place you won't forget. Brewmasters and owners Chris Pearson and Bob Lusin decided that after being in the same home brewing club, they wanted to start a brewery. Expect creations and experimentations with recipes that go beyond the traditional style norms.

OWNER
Steve Carter, Chris Pearson, Bob Lusin, Mark Mileusnic

HEAD BREWER
Chris Pearson, Bob Lusin

AVAILABILITY
IN

BEST KNOWN FOR
IPAs, stouts

DATE FOUNDED
2014

2017 PRODUCTION
400 bbl

KEY EVENTS
Heaven's Court Day (Jun)

11 | 60 | • | • | | • | | | • | | 4.1/5

THE DEVIL'S TRUMPET BREWING CO.

PRO TIPS

» Dog friendly on the patio only.

» If available, try one of their sours or barrel-conditioned beers.

» They offer a beer sampler called Flight of the 11 (all 11 beers on draft), a great option for first timers. But don't worry, that's only about 2.75 pints in volume.

» In the summer they have a beautiful patio and sometimes a food truck if you get hungry! Otherwise, they are bring in your own food.

» Just down the street from the Albanese Candy Factory. Pair your beers with some gummy bears.

DATE OF VISIT:

MY RATING
☆ ☆ ☆ ☆ ☆

NOTES:

POPULAR BEERS

M	Tu	W	Th	F	S	Su
3-9p	3-9p	3-9p	3-9p	3-11p	12-11p	12-8p

NEW OBERPFALZ BREWING

FIELD NOTES

The Oberpfalz region of Bavaria is where the head brewer of New Oberpfalz's family is from, so giving a shout back to the area, bordering the Czech Republic and north of Munich, made sense when starting up this Indiana brewery. Releasing their first brews in 2015, New Oberpfalz specializes in German-style ales and lagers, but works outwards from there to encompass a variety of styles popular to American craft beer fans. New Oberpfalz' flagships are a pale, Helles lager, and a Schwarzbier.

121 E. Main St.
Griffith, IN 46319
219-513-9341
newoberpfalz.com

OWNER
Dan Lehnerer,
Jennifer Lehnerer

HEAD BREWER
Dan Lehnerer

AVAILABILITY
IN

BEST KNOWN FOR
Lagers, IPAs, stouts

DATE FOUNDED
2015

2017 PRODUCTION
429 bbl

KEY EVENTS
Crawfish Boil (May),
Oktoberfest (Sept)

| 12 | 75 | • | • | • | | | • | • | | 4.1/5 |

NEW OBERPFALZ BREWING

PRO TIPS

» Dog friendly on the patio only.

» New Oberpfalz does distribute their beer, but not over the state line. So if you want packaged beer, be prepared to drive to Indiana.

» The brewpub is a quaint, unassuming space on Griffith's main drag that offers around a dozen different house-made beers on draft and in bottle form.

» Picnic tables with sun umbrellas grace the patio when the weather cooperates.

» The menu offers a selection of appetizers, sandwiches, and personal-sized pizzas. The weisswurst is a lovely take on the German-style encased meat served on a pretzel roll.

DATE OF VISIT:

MY RATING
☆ ☆ ☆ ☆ ☆

NOTES:

POPULAR BEERS

M	Tu	W	Th	F	S	Su
closed	3-10p	3-10p	3-10p	11a-10p	11a-10p	11a-7p

POKRO BREWING COMPANY

FIELD NOTES

Classic story here - head brewer and founder Joe Pokropinski (hence the name) has been brewing for over a decade and a half. He began, like many brewers do, with homebrewing. Getting a push from his wife Robyn, who's the business brains of the operation, the pair began this labor of love which culminated in a Valentine's Day 2015 opening. Pokropinski's beers focus on American, English, and Belgian styles, with enough variety on the modest list to keep you from getting bored with the options.

311 N. Broad St.
Griffith, IN 46319
219-924-7950
pokrobrewing.com

OWNER
Joe Pokropinski,
Robyn Pokropinski

HEAD BREWER
Joe Pokropinski

AVAILABILITY
NW IN

BEST KNOWN FOR
Belgian, English

DATE FOUNDED
2015

KEY EVENTS
POKtoberfest (Oct)

12 | 100 | | | • | | • | • | | 4.0/5

POKRO BREWING COMPANY

PRO TIPS

» The back room of the taproom space advertises "a man-cave feel with jukebox, board games, giant Jenga, boards & bags, vintage multicade, and dartboard."

» Pokro hosts a variety of events at its space, including a painting-and-drinking night, a musical open-mic night, and even a pop-up boutique.

» There is a food menu available, featuring Polish-inspired cuisine, including pierogi, golabki, sausages, and other favorites.

» If you're feeling a little hair of the dog, Pokro offers to turn any brew on the menu into a beer-mosa with a splash (or more if you want it) of orange juice.

DATE OF VISIT:

MY RATING
☆ ☆ ☆ ☆ ☆

NOTES:

POPULAR BEERS

 | Monkey Assasin | Caveman Ale | Cammit!

M	Tu	W	Th	F	S	Su
closed	2-10p	2-10p	2-11p	2p-12a	12p-12a	12-8p

ST. JOHN MALT BROS. BREWERY&EATERY

FIELD NOTES

9607 Wicker Ave.
St. John, IN 46373
219-627-4294
sjmaltbros.com

St. John Malt Brother's story began during a snow blizzard on February 1, 2015 when they opened their doors to a small crowd on Super Bowl Sunday. This 36-person capacity taproom quickly gained the reputation of brewing great beer with great service. In January 2018, they expanded their kitchen facilities and now offer a full food menu. Additionally, they broadened their self-distribution market to include Northern Indiana, Indianapolis, Lafayette and Illinois.

OWNER
Jim Estry, Dan Cox,
Dave Witt

HEAD BREWER
Dan Breed

AVAILABILITY
IN, IL

BEST KNOWN FOR
IPAs, porters,
stouts, browns, BA
specialties

DATE FOUNDED
2015

2017 PRODUCTION
574 bbl

KEY EVENTS
Ribfest (May), Luau
(Aug)

16 | 47 | • | | | • | | • | • | | 3.9/5

ST. JOHN MALT BROS. BREWERY&EATERY

PRO TIPS

» The inside of the taproom is friendly with some bar seating, but most will be accommodated at the tables of various heights. Some outdoor seating is available on two patios.

» The taproom itself is only open Fridays and Saturdays from 5p-10p while the "Eatery" is only 7 days a week.

» Bombers and cans of some beers can be had at the pub. All beer, to-go or otherwise, is $2 off on Tuesdays, and growlers are $3 off on Sundays.

» Live music; follow them on Twitter for announcements.

» Wine and craft sodas are available.

DATE OF VISIT:

MY RATING
☆ ☆ ☆ ☆ ☆

NOTES:

POPULAR BEERS

M	Tu	W	Th	F	S	Su
3-11p	3-11p	3-11p	3-11p	2p-12a	11a-12a	11a-9p

WILDROSE BREWING

FIELD NOTES

Wildrose Brewing is built out of a large, re-purposed pole barn space by five friends who bonded over a love of homebrewing in their own garages. Sharing the beers with friends (who must have responded favorably) led to the idea that they should start their own operation, and, well, here we are. Wildrose opened in Griffith, IN in 2015, less than a mile from fellow brewers Pokro and New Oberpfalz. Stouts and hops dominate the draft menu here, with the occasional pilsner and wheat ale peeking through.

1104 E. Main St.
Griffith, IN 46319
219-595-5054
wildrosebrewing.com

OWNER
Kevin Krippel,
Tony Nicola, Karen
DeJong, David
DeJong

DATE FOUNDED
2014

HEAD BREWER
David DeJong

AVAILABILITY
NW IN

BEST KNOWN FOR
IPAs, pales, stouts,
wheat ales

12 | 100 | • | • | | • | | • | • | | 3.9/5

WILDROSE BREWING

PRO TIPS

» Dog friendly on the patio only.

» Roses, thorns, and skulls adorn the front of the Wildrose facility like it was a long lost hard rock album cover from the 1980s.

» There's a shaded patio perfect for the sunniest of summer days when you've forgotten your sunblock.

» The food menu is small but adequate, featuring sandwiches, burgers, and appetizers all meant to soak up a bit of the booze and raise your blood pressure ever so slightly.

» Live music on Fridays.

» Don't overlook the guest cider on draft.

DATE OF VISIT:

MY RATING
☆ ☆ ☆ ☆ ☆

NOTES:

POPULAR BEERS

Big Sexy | Mad Cow | Mornin' James | Hop Side Of The Moon

M	Tu	W	Th	F	S	Su
3-11p	3-11p	3-11p	3-11p	3p-12a	12p-12a	12-8p

WINDMILL BREWING

FIELD NOTES

2121 Gettler St.
Dyer, IN 46311
219-440-2189
windmillbrew.com

Windmills are often seen as a national symbol of The Netherlands, where they were used for everything from scooping and draining the wetlands to grinding grain to flour in mills. In Dyer, IN, the Windmill is also the symbol of Scott Vander Griend and Justin Verburg, two friends of Dutch extraction, who, after years of years of friendship and homebrewing, decided to start Windmill Brewing in 2015. Their goal is to offer craft beer fans brews that aren't necessarily assaults on the palate, but a wide range of balanced flavors that continually push tradition instead.

OWNER
Scott Vander Griend, Justin Verburg

HEAD BREWER
Justin, Verburg

AVAILABILITY
NW IN

BEST KNOWN FOR
Belgians, IPAs, pales, stouts

DATE FOUNDED
2015

2017 PRODUCTION
300 bbl

KEY EVENTS
Anniversary Party (Aug)

14 | 55 | | • | | | | | • | | 4.1/5

WINDMILL BREWING

PRO TIPS

» There's a three beer per person per day limit at Windmill, so keep that in mind when examining their list of 8-10 beers.

» Cans to-go are usually available on site, but check ahead for up to date availability.

» The space itself is small-ish, but charming, with a couple bar seats, a chalkboard draft list, stamped metal tables and a characterful mix of chairs.

» A giant Jenga game set is featured prominently in the taproom.

» Keep your eye out for the brewery's cat, Luther. He's quite popular.

» Watch for variant releases of their hugely popular Memesicle series "milk shake" IPAs.

POPULAR BEERS

Memesicle Milk-shake IPAs	Mosaic Tessellation	Pale Dutch Boy	40 Hulking Giants

M	Tu	W	Th	F	S	Su
3-10p	3-10p	3-10p	3-10p	3-11p	11a-11p	closed

DATE OF VISIT:

MY RATING
☆ ☆ ☆ ☆ ☆

NOTES:

INDEX